D1088290

FRANCESCA PRINA

The Story of
GOTHIC ARCHITECTURE

PRESTEL

Munich · London · New York

CONTENTS

5 **INTRODUCTION**

22 **THE MAIN CHARACTERISTICS OF A NEW STYLE**
36 Origins of Gothic Architecture: the Île-de-France
38 Cistercian Architecture
40 Early English: the first English Gothic Architecture
42 Canterbury Cathedral

44 **HIGH GOTHIC**
56 The Chartres Model
58 The Territories of the German Empire
60 Strasbourg Cathedral
62 Cologne Cathedral
64 Hanseatic Cities and the Baltic
66 Lübeck
68 The French Midi
70 The Papal Palace in Avignon
71 Albi Cathedral
72 Carcassonne
74 The Kingdom of Castile
75 Burgos Cathedral
76 English Decorated Gothic
78 Chapter Houses
80 York Minister
82 Italy

86 Upper Church of the Basilica of St Francis, Assisi, Italy
88 Palazzi Pubblici, Loggias and Markets
92 Venice
93 The Dodge's Palace
94 Sienna
95 Sienna Cathedral
96 The Castles of Frederick II

98 **THE FINAL YEARS OF THE MIDDLE AGES**
104 Prague: The Founding of an Imperial City
106 St Vitus's Cathedral
108 An Architectural Dynasty: The Parler family
112 The Cathedral, Milan
114 Cracow and Poland
118 English Perpendicular
120 King's College Chapel, Cambridge
122 Westminster Abbey, Henry VII's Chapel
124 Flanders and Brabant
126 Bruges
128 France Private Dwellings (Hôtels)
130 Catalonia and Aragon
134 Isabelline Gothic in Spain
138 Manueline Architecture in Portugal
140 The Convent of Santa Maria da Vitoria, Batalha

142 Index of Places

143 Photographic Credits

INTRODUCTION

Shortly before the middle of the 12th century, a radical transformation of Romanesque forms in the Île-de-France led to the creation of a new architectural style; namely Gothic. This genre of architecture would eventually spread to the whole of Europe, and even beyond, by the mid-15th century. Indeed, between the 12th and 15th centuries, Western Europe experienced an era of extraordinary urban development, the result of economic and demographic growth and development. Just as the spread of Romanesque architecture had occurred in a period of reorganization and expansion after the end of the barbarian invasions and the weakening of Islamic pressure, so the Gothic style developed in the context of political stability. Noteworthy among the distinctive characteristics of this period were the creation of the great nation states: France under Louis VI, the reorganisation of the German Empire under the Hohenstaufen dynasty, the southward expansion of the Christian kingdoms — the Reconquest — in the Iberian peninsula, the birth of the Italian republics as well as the Flemish merchant cities.

Thus a universal language of architectural forms, utilised by western Christendom — with some influences deriving from the Crusades, the Venetian companies and the activity of the northern military formations in Slavo-Byzantine Europe — emerged around 1140 with the rebuilding of the abbatial church of Saint-Denis, near Paris. Building sites sprung up all across Europe. A new artistic sensibility spread from the architecture of the French cathedrals, the outcome of philosophical and religious ideas engendered by the speculations of the intellectuals and the elevation of the status of Notre Dame, Our Virgin. Furthermore, as the result of technical and formal advances in order to achieve an extremely high nave, new architectural principles developed.

Origins and developments of sacred architecture

Since the majority of Gothic monuments were religious buildings, the architecture of this period was interpreted according to its religious and symbolic meanings. Medieval texts of a theological, liturgical, didactic or mystical nature frequently dwelt on the notion of a religious building as being the 'house of God', a symbol of His intangible substance, with temporal images of Paradise and of heavenly Jerusalem. Gothic churches provide a formal and a tangible basis to this idea in the vast scale and the incredible height of the cathedrals, as well as in the incredible lightness of the walls, which allowed

Cathedral of Notre-Dame, Paris, 1163–1330

Notre-Dame Cathedral — the first cathedral constructed of monumental proportions — is seen as the place where heaven and earth meet; a reflection of divine grandeur. The specific link between the great Parisian cathedral and the Capetian monarchy is made evident by the frieze of French kings above the three doorways, known as the Gallery of Kings. The original statues of the kings, which were badly damaged during the Revolution, are now kept in the Musée de Cluny in Paris.

diffuse, abundant light to enter the space, like the grace of God. The illuminating windows were compared to the precious stones in the walls of the heavenly Jerusalem; the towers recalled those in the vision of St John. To these elements the iconography of sculpture, imagery and stained glass windows were added, arranged in an instructive or mystical series imbued with cosmic symbolism.

The Île-de-France series of cathedrals — and those of the north of France generally — are especially homogeneous and structurally sophisticated. Notre-Dame in Paris is perhaps the most well-known example. However, the following phase of French Gothic derived from Laon, coinciding with the triumphant reign of Philip Augustus (1179–1223), during which, in an astonishing architectural crescendo, the series of 'classic' Gothic masterpieces — Chartres, Rheims, Amiens, Noyon and Soissons — were all constructed. The spread of

opposite page
The nave of Westminster Abbey, London, 1258–1269, completed post-1375

Built at the behest of King Henry III, who financed it almost completely from his own purse, Westminster Abbey represents a unique case in the history of medieval English architecture. The abbey was initially intended as the tomb of Edward the Confessor (canonised in 1161), in an attempt to strengthen the position of the English monarchy. It is for this reason that it is perhaps the most 'French' of the great English churches. The abbey is remarkable due to its height (32m/105 ft) and its sumptuous ornamentation throughout, rather like a huge reliquary. Westminster Abbey paved the way for the Decorated Style.

this page
Choir of basilica of Vézelay Abbey (St Mary Magdalene), 1185, France

The choir in Vézelay is the first incursion of the Île-de-France Gothic style into the Burgundy region. 'Light' in both senses of the word, the choir displays its modernity in the prominent linearity of the shafts that support the ribs of the vaults and surround the pillars of the ambulatory. A further innovation was the removal of the upper section of the dividing walls between the chapels, which allows more light to be admitted into the space.

opposite page
**The choir of Aachen cathedral,
c. 1355, Germany**

The further one advances into the
13th and 14th centuries, the more
one sees how interior walls and
partitions were eliminated in Gothic
buildings in order to emphasise the
spatial continuity between interior
and exterior. The influence of Cologne
Cathedral and the Sainte-Chapelle
in Paris can be perceived in the
design of the choir of Aachen Cathedral, a light and spacious showcase
for flaunting the spoils of King
Charlemagne. Masonry structure
was reduced to the bare minimum
necessary and serves solely as a
framework for the enormous windows.

left
**The crossing of Noyon Cathedral,
second half of the 12th century,
France**

The linearity of early French Gothic
reached its culmination at Noyon
Cathedral, where a marked sense
of verticality carries through the four
levels of the elevation, introducing
clusters of upward-thrusting shafts.
Fragmenting the masonry produces
an effect of lightness and transparency, enhanced by the increase in
brightness from bottom to top.

French Gothic was confined, at first, to the territories of the French crown. The
building of cathedrals, which increased the crown's prestige and made its
power apparent, accompanied the expansionist policy of the kingdom. The
focus of this ripple effect was the city of Paris, the unquestioned capital and
cultural centre, from where French Gothic expanded northwards and south-
wards.

The 'French method' of building was adopted by other European countries to
become a common stylistic aesthetic at that time. England, with its historic
links to France, welcomed the 'French method of working' quite some time
before other European countries. Highly interesting variations of the French
method were introduced at the same time, which were connected with its
particular liturgical tradition, its processional worship and its cult of relics. Indeed, its history, notable for its centuries-old conflicts with France, is reflected in its loyalty to 10th–11th century Anglo-Norman construction methods,
borrowing from the formal repertoire of French architecture only those elements which could be reconciled with its traditional forms. English Gothic
architecture can be broadly subdivided into three phases which do not corre-
spond to the definitions of the Early, High and Late Gothic used for continental architecture: Early English Gothic between 1170 and 1240, Decorated
Gothic between 1240 and c. 1330 and Perpendicular between 1330 and
approximately late 15th century.

In Spain, the construction of three great cathedrals — Burgos, Toledo and León — took place rapidly in the 1220s. The forms of the cathedrals strictly following the French models, although not without characteristics and stylistic variants which would achieve full maturity during the following century. In fact, the history of Gothic architecture in Iberia coincided with the different historic conditions to which the various partly independent kingdoms were subject up until the 15th century — hence the spatial experimentation in Catalonia or even the incredible development of Catalan-Aragonese secular architecture. It was only in the late 15th century, with the unification of the kingdoms of Castile and Aragon, that a Spanish courtly style developed from the encounter between European Late Gothic forms, *mudejar* decoration and isolated Renaissance motifs took the form, not only of a rapid sequence of cathedrals, but also in the erection of hospitals and colleges.

However, Portuguese architecture took its architectural leap from Romanesque to Gothic forms rather late, with the construction of the monastery of Batalha in 1385. This monastery was not only an architectural symbol of the Aviz dynasty, but also — because it was continually added to — a kind of manual of Portuguese Gothic architecture, a domain for experimentation and the prototype for all the important commissions of the country. The subsequent 'Manueline architecture', although already modern in its representational programme of dynastic propaganda, nevertheless took its formal idiom from European Late Gothic.

Germanic regions first accepted French Gothic with considerable reluctance in a simplified and sporadic way; the cathedrals of Strasbourg and Cologne being isolated exceptions. The Holy Roman Empire continued to present a politically and culturally diverse background, reaching from the Baltic to Sicily at a time when French Gothic architecture became the inspiration for new

Exterior of Seville Cathedral, 1401–1519, Spain

Seville Cathedral plays an important role in the evolution of Spanish cathedrals that developed elements of French and English origin. A quintessential political and religious monument, Seville Cathedral manifests a clear ambition to surpass all earlier buildings both in its sheer dimensions and in the abundance of its decoration. The patrons who commissioned the cathedral wanted it to reflect their elite social status in Seville. The project was also an opportunity to confront and challenge international architectural culture, as was the case with the Visconti/Sforza cathedral in Milan, built in the same period.

**Campanile of Santa Maria del Fiore,
1334–1360, Florence**

Giotto's initial design for the bell tower of Florence's cathedral envisaged
a slender parallelepiped culminating
in a prominent spire, clad with white,
green and dark red marble. On the
death of the artist in 1337, Andrea
Pisano and Francesco Talenti modified
Giotto's design due to a number of
structural and functional concerns.
However, Pisano and Talenti did not
discard the original aesthetic, but
rather doubled up the original plans
for two-and three-light mullioned windows at each level together with twisted torsos creating a new sort of balcony feature. The result is a pleasant
combination, a Cosmati aesthetic with
a touch of the classical that was
already present in the Florentine
architecture of the day.

Choir of Beauvais Cathedral, begun 1225, rebuilt 1284, France

If the verticality of Gothic architecture derives from the combination of new construction techniques, it is equally true that the quest for spectacular buildings, testing the limits of structural possibilities, was also the result of municipal rivalries. The height of each new cathedral was indeed higher than preceding ones: 24m in Laon, 32.5m in Paris, 42m in Amiens, 47.5m in Beauvais.

In 1284, a most devastating accident occurred on a Gothic construction site: due to its extraordinary height and structural fragility, the choir of Beauvais Cathedral (begun about 1225 and finished in 1272), collapsed under the force of the wind. The choir would be rebuilt differently from the original design.

This calamity signalled the end of an era. Both builders and clients abandoned the aspiration for ever-greater height, which had hitherto been the mark of the chief experiments in Gothic architecture.

commissions. From the 14th to the 15th century, thanks to a process set in motion by members of the Parler family, German Gothic evolved towards the late forms of ever more sophisticated decoration.

In Italy, however, Gothic architecture for cathedrals developed at a slower pace and with different characteristics, thanks to a strong Romanesque tradition and Italy's deep classical roots. Even then, with the first hints of cisalpine Gothic and the break with Romanesque structures (during the late 13th century) masonry never lost its overt load-bearing role. Italy is indeed the country that interpreted the Gothic style only in a minor way in its original form as mediated through the work of Cistercian craftsmen.

In the panorama of religious architecture in Europe, the buildings of the religious orders hold a relatively important position. Although there existed several Benedictine foundations in Normandy and England, the Dominicans and Franciscans treated the Gothic style in a unique way, concentrating their monasteries in cities. Whilst during the 13th century the extraordinary spread of Cistercians throughout Europe was a valuable means of disseminating Gothic architecture.

Secular architecture

European Gothic architecture was not limited to, or only represented symbolically, by religious buildings but was also used in secular buildings. Statistics indicate an exponential increase in the population of Europe between the mid-12th and early 14th centuries. Population growth, the development of manufacturing and commerce — and the subsequent flourishing and signifi-

above left
Arnolfo di Cambio, Palazzo Vecchio, c. 1299, Florence

The Palazzo Vecchio, with its inner courtyard, combines the typology of a military building with the functionality of a grand public building. The asymmetric position of the tower marks it out as the visual hub of the city.

above right
Les Halles (Cloth Market), late 13th century — 1486, Bruges, Belgium

In Flemish, the word *halle* meant the space dedicated to trading or to warehouses. It was also a suitable meeting place for the community. The public function of the cloth market is indicated by the high tower, which highlights the fusion of urban, feudal and religious architectural elements in a single entity.

cance of cities — meant that the most important towns became strategic political centres, where imperial meetings, councils or corporate assemblies were held, consequently expanding the roles of administration and representation.

Civil architecture thus went beyond being purely functional in character, competing conceptually with ecclesiastical and feudal architecture, adopting and creating its own elements and symbolism in aristocratic palaces; the influence of the building sites of the great cathedrals is evident. The birth of a typically urban architecture signalled the transformation of a feudal, agrarian society into an urban, bourgeois society. From the 13th century the great orthogonal block of the town hall, a building typical of the new aristocracy, replaced older houses, altering the pattern of city streets and defining the urban image, as the hierarchy of the social order illustrated. Although the cathedral remained the most significant building in cities where a bishop ruled, in socially more advanced cities the town hall was constructed nearby. The assumption of new powers by the city authorities required the construction of showpiece buildings as well as offices for the administration of public

preceding page
Hôtel-Dieu, 1443, Beaune, France

The hospice at Beaune, founded by Chancellor Nicolas Rolin from Burgundy, was intended to alleviate the suffering of the citizens in the famine consequent to the Hundred Years' War. The rooms are arranged round a courtyard with a timber gallery.

Pedro Salvá, Bellver Castle, 1309–1314, Palma de Mallorca, Spain

A defensive military building and summer residence of the Majorcan monarchs, the castle consists of a main block with a circular floor plan, flanked by two towers, built round an inner courtyard that allows light into the inner rooms through two levels of arcades.

affairs. The town hall thus became an important building and was frequently built on the square in front of the cathedral, being positioned as a counterpoint: a kind of juxtaposition of conflicting concepts of sacred and secular architecture. A symbolic language of self-representation of the populace developed, whereby different typologies, functions and spatial programmes evolved depending on whether it was a thriving trading city in northern Europe or a proud commune in southern Europe. In the regions of Flanders and Brabant, the rapid growth of international trade — commercial, manufacturing, banking as well as artistic and cultural — had already strongly stimulated civic life from the end of the 13th century, from where the full development of the public building sector ensued.

In Italy, the proliferation of prestigious buildings for the communal judiciary testified to the attention that both the clients and the authorities in charge gave to the quality of urban space — new tools were adopted for town-planning — as well as to decoration. Thus a whole range of public structures built in central and northern Italy after 1250 bear witness to a thriving communal life. These buildings are marked by an expression of openness to the world by

Guy de Dammartin, wall of the fireplace in the Grande Salle, c. 1386, Poitiers Courthouse, France

During courtly occasions, one wall of the sumptuous room in the residence of Duc Jean de Berry formed an ingenious theatrical backdrop. At the top of a flight of steps and devised as a proscenium, the fireplace serves as a kind of stage under the musicians' gallery above it.

The glazed wall above is divided into several superimposed levels in a sophisticated play of punctured walls, to create the rarefied and opulent atmosphere of late Gothic courts.

the use of wide colonnades on the ground floor and large windows and loggias with external stairs to the upper floor that eliminated virtually any military elements from these buildings (an exception being the Palazzo Vecchio
in Florence).

Moreover, spaces of this kind communicated specific political messages, as is
reflected in the careful choice of decoration for the façades. Whereas in the
course of the 14th century the town halls of Hanseatic cities like Lübeck and
Bremen were adorned with a multitude of sculptures of the emperor and the
electors, the free Italian municipalities decorated their public buildings with
the emblems of the various city magistrates and allied authorities. In the
realm of secular architecture, buildings that housed commercial activities
were of great importance to the community: the cloth markets of Brabant and
Flanders were among the most impressive examples of urban development
created during that period. Their majestic and often expensive, high-quality
architecture emphasised the importance of this commercial activity, above
all in the great trading centres of Brabant and Flanders, which were based on
the export of textiles. In some instances, their buildings also housed the communal administration and took over the city tower — the symbol of the legal
status of the urban community. Thanks to their economic power Brabant and
Flanders were independent, appropriating the role of dominance from the
stately tower — a typology of building particular to the northern regions.

There was an equally intense fervour to build castles and fortified houses,
which the courts and centres of feudal power required due to the highly un-

Half-timbered houses, 15th century, Colmar, France

Residential buildings in central and
northern Europe used a construction
technique based on load-bearing
timber frames filled with panels made
of various materials mixed in variable
proportions. Half-timbering is dis-
cernible in the façade of the timber-
framed structure that, thanks to the
use of vertical posts extending from
ground to roof, replaced the construction of separate, independent storeys
during the late Middle Ages. The use
of shorter posts, arranged with an eye
to aesthetic quality, also enabled an
increase in height.

Casa Isolani, 13th century, Bologna, Italy

The manner in which the upper floors protrude on wooden structures is typical of medieval buildings. The use of these overhangs allowed the potential building area to be maximised or colonnades to be built along the street, with (work)shops beneath. Still supported by its high wooden beams, Casa Isolani is a rare example of a 13th century private dwelling. On the ground floor, the arcade opens on to communal areas, while the upper level, intended to accommodate the private quarters, is lit by three double-pane windows.

stable political and social context. The contrast and the attempt at integration and compromise between defensive and residential buildings is clearly exemplified in the characteristic evolution of the medieval fortress. On the one hand the desire for conquest, the assertion and the expansion of power motivated the continual updating of techniques of war thus dictating the constant development of systems of defence. On the other hand, considerations of prestige and leadership imposed an 'appropriate' lifestyle in grand castles and magnificent houses. Military architecture, particularly castles and princely residences, was often imbued with the ideals of chivalry and was notable for aristocratic ostentation. In the course of the 14th century, fortresses gradually ceased to look like strategic, defensive buildings, allowing their residential function to come to the fore as theatres of splendid and luxurious courtly life.

Private dwellings had a specific layout and were far more modest than public buildings in the late Middle Ages. In accordance with urban development in the medieval city typified by narrow winding streets, laid out — at least initially — in an *ad hoc* manner, the buildings adhered to the classic medieval cadastral messuage: a long, narrow rectangle with a narrow courtyard in the middle. The houses were usually built on three floors: the trading premises were on the ground floor facing the street; the kitchen was at the rear, if possible overlooking a little garden; a staircase led to the upper floors, where the family lived and to the lofts used for grain, store rooms and wood stores. The small dimension of the space was dictated by the need to light the interior adequately and to keep it warm. The windows, at least at first, were not glazed but were only protected by sheets of waxed paper or parchment, which allowed very little light into the interior. Due to the high cost, leaded lights were rare and were only reserved for the important rooms. Given the desire of the merchant class to have comfortable abodes, the burgher's house developed fairly early on. Initially these houses were built of timber, but later due to frequent fires, stone was used; or bricks if stone was lacking.

Architecture and the builder's yard

One is prone to focusing on the theological, metaphoric and symbolic message of Gothic architecture, overlooking the fact that constructing these masterpieces needed extraordinary manual and organisational competence. As Gothic architecture has always been admired as a *chef d'œuvre* of technological achievement, the identity and works of master builders are mentioned more and more frequently in documents from the 12th century onwards. The architect played the most important role on the building site, he took responsibility of the planning as well as the practical economic organisation and

Villard de Honnecourt, plan for the tower of Laon Cathedral, c. 1230 –1240, Bibliothèque Nationale, Paris

Villard de Honnecourt's fame is due to the publication of his *Book of Portraiture*, an annotated sketchbook illustrating architectural techniques used on Gothic construction sites. The notebook contains about 250 drawings illustrating the principal aspects of theory and practice in the professional training of a medieval architect: from carpentry and machines used on site, to sculptural models and concepts of geometry and proportion executed with set square and compass.

management of the works. He was set apart from the workers, as he would have had solely executive tasks to perform. The architect acquired his skills mainly on the job, yet consciously employed a number of rules based on geometrically derived proportion. Due to the ambition of those who commissioned the work and the competition between various construction yards, many architects travelled in order to study the best architectural examples. There were numerous stages of construction and planning: the plans were drawn by the architect to be approved by the authorities, after which there was the implementation phase when construction itself finally commenced. To organise and administrate the construction process an independent organisation was set up called the *'opus, opera'* or 'works', which handled the finances, managed the workforce and signed the contracts. The great builders' yards of the cathedrals and palaces acquired considerable importance, not only as a source of employment, but also for the vast network of interests which they created around them and which influenced the realms of both production and commerce, from the manufacture of the materials (e.g. bricks and lime) to the quarrying of the stone or the felling of the trees. Thus, these yards assumed a notable economic and social importance in the medieval city.

Building site, from the *Roman des Girart de Rousillon*, cod. 2554, vol. 164, second half of the 15th century, Austrian National Library, Vienna, Austria

In order to construct a great building, workers with a very wide range of skills were required. Many unqualified workers were recruited for the foundations, while the masonry needed mainly skilled stonecutters and masons.

The fascinating world of the building site is recreated in this miniature, which illustrates the different phases of the work, from mixing the cement and the placing of the ashlars, down to the work of dressing the stone. It was an itinerant workforce as it was linked both to the availability of funds and to the presence of an architect.

THE MAIN CHARACTERISTICS
OF A NEW STYLE

The distinctive features of Gothic architecture are not an absolute novelty in the European panorama of art, rather they are the conclusion of a series of previous developments and the solution of several problems left unresolved by the earlier Romanesque style. The employment of a very high central nave and the distinct verticality of load-bearing structures, for example, were inherited from previous architectural trends — from the great Ottoman structures down to Clunic buildings. Nevertheless, the transformation of the Romanesque church into the Gothic entailed a long and gradual process of conversion from a structural emphasis to a diametrically opposed aesthetic and formal emphasis such as the type of roofing, the articulation of supports and the plans and elevations.

The mechanism of subdivision, the balancing and the channelling of forces at work within the building structure render Gothic architecture dynamic and flexible rather than static and rigid as with Romanesque architecture. In the new building projects of that time, the massive walls of the Romanesque church, with unbroken walls pierced by small, widely-spaced windows are slowly transformed into a completely different structure; where the wall plane all but vanishes, filigree and translucent and adorned with intricate stained glass windows.

The manner in which the architectural transformation of the Romanesque into the Gothic is effected, is by replacing a structural system of thick walls and heavy masses with a structure free from any unnecessary elements. The wonderful lightness and brightness of the Gothic cathedral lies in stark contrast to the dim, sombre light of the Romanesque church.

**External view of the choir and apse,
Canterbury Cathedral, 1174–1184, England**

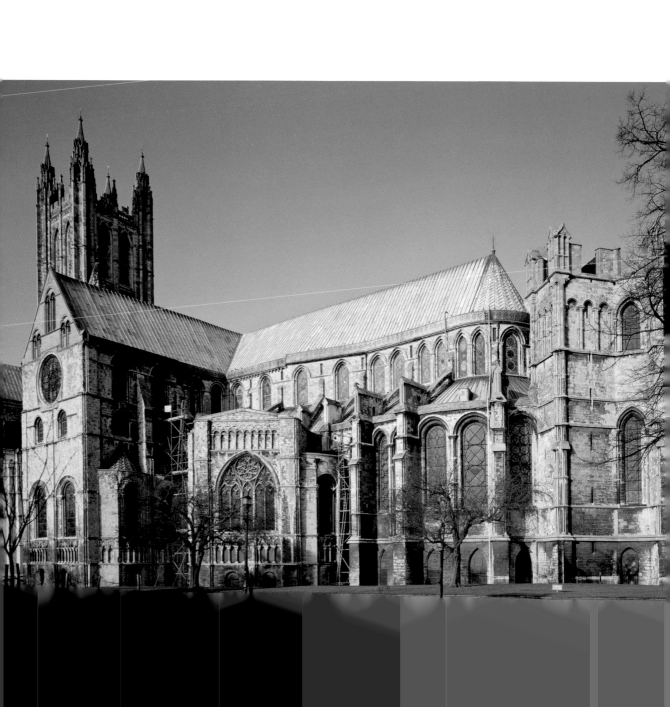

External view, Romanesque church of Sainte-Foy, mid-11th century, Conques, France

The external articulation of the choir at the church of Sainte-Foy reveals a double divide — horizontal and vertical — of the ambulatory chapels and of the apse in a superimposition of volumes typical of Romanesque architecture that highlights the function of different spaces. Whereas in Gothic cathedrals, on the other hand, the apsidal arrangement conceals the internal structure beneath a mass of buttresses, pinnacles and finials. All elements which do not contribute to the structural stability of the building are eliminated in order to emphasise the vertical slenderness, i.e. the sphere of the Divine. This emphasis tends to stress the importance of the glass surfaces, which are no longer merely small, single lights but rather huge, high windows enriched with stained glass.

The Cathedral

Gothic cathedrals generally have a Latin-cross plan, with three or five aisles and a more or less prominent transept (the space across the nave which gives the cruciform shape). Lengthwise the axis lies east-west, with the altar at the eastern end orientated towards the rising sun. The choir is situated alongside an ambulatory and radial chapels. However, there are noteworthy differences in plan layout of Gothic cathedrals depending on the region: in the region of Paris, cathedrals do not generally have transepts though might have wings projecting only a short distance from the nave (Bourges and Paris), while cathedrals in the region of Noyon and Soisson in Picardy have complex plans and massive transepts. English cathedrals, on the other hand, are characterised by extremely long basilica-like plans with projecting transepts (occasionally double as at Salisbury Cathedral) and square choirs (except at Westminster Abbey and Canterbury Cathedral) with an especially prominent eastern end (retrochoir) — the so-called Lady Chapel — dedicated to honouring the Virgin. These chapels — where monks and priests celebrate a daily Mass in Mary's honour — were built onto the north side of the choir and became a common feature from the early 12th century.

 The harmony of the proportions and the lightness of the cathedral developed in two different directions: the vertical dimension (symbol of reaching out to the Divine) is carried to its climactic expression in the tower, while the longitudinal dimension, dependent on the structural design, is frequently composed of parts which blend with each other in a free and varied sequence. The specific nature of a Gothic cathedral is determined by the shape of the great central nave, designed to great heights with a variable breadth-to-height ratio (from 1:2 to 1:3.5) to create a space punctuated by the mod-

Exterior, Gothic choir of
Saint-Etienne's cathedral, 1284,
Beauvais, France

Floor plan of a Romanesque cathedral compared with a floor plan of a Gothic cathedral

The Romanesque plan layout is a simple Latin cross form with a broad projecting transept (1), three naves (2) and external apses consisting of three chapels in series (3). The alternation of supports — columns and piers (4) — results in double bays for the nave (5) compared with the two aisles.

As with the Romanesque plan, the plan of a Gothic cathedral is frequently a Latin cross form, however the transept does not project far (6) (or may even be absent). The plan generally consists of a nave and double aisles (7) supported on piers. The apse configuration in the chancel is complex (8). The choir is encircled by a double apse (9), known as the ambulatory, from which numerous radial chapels (10) fan out.

A comparison of the two plans alongside one another illustrates firstly the mono-directional movement through the Romanesque building from west end to altar and secondly the multi-directional possibilities of the Gothic cathedral which allows the faithful to choose different routes through the space.

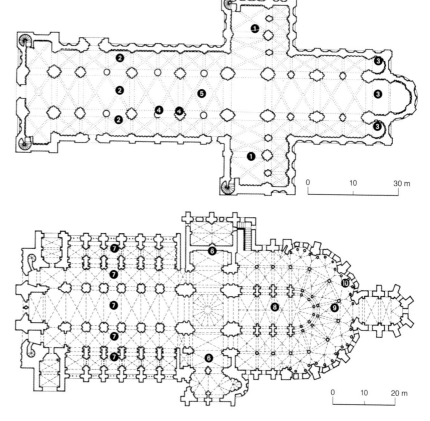

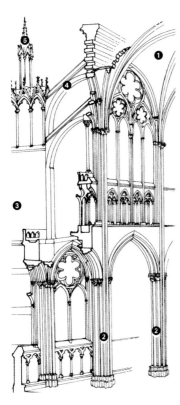

Cross-section, Saint-Denis, France

The structural functionalism of Gothic architecture is illustrated primarily in the ribbed vaulting (1) and the clustered piers (2). The load of the roof causes localised point loads that the structural design neutralises by counterthrusts and the calculated vertical weights in solid buttresses (3), flying buttresses (4) and finials (5). It is a dynamic and flexible system, insofar as it tolerates distortion in the walls due to ground settlement or weather conditions.

above right
Flying buttresses, Cathedral of Notre-Dame, c. 1194–1221, Chartres, France

The flying buttress developed in Gothic architecture as an external strut system positioned above the roof structure of the aisles. The arches of the choir in Chartres are concentric arcs linked by small radial columns to reflect the large dimensions of the choir.

ular rhythm of the bay, where light is utilised both physically and metaphorically to emphasise the structural and logical processes that underlie the architecture. All these components contribute to the dissolution of the wall plane — 'diaphanous process' — where the autonomy of the different structural parts is limited in favour of a greater spatial fusion and multiple lines of sight, which give a pleasing three-dimensional, spatial effect. The Gothic space is not geometrically defined or enclosed, but rather is it a space conceived and transformed by the play of light — a coloured light, filtered through the stained glass windows, not a neutral light, far removed from the Romanesque.

Spires, pinnacles, gables and flying buttresses play a central role in the aesthetic and formal aspects of a Gothic building; the buttresses break up the external volumetric areas into a kind of kaleidoscopic composition. The Gothic cathedral is the expression of an urban civilisation: it is indicative of the desire for presentation in a lofty, beautiful church, the ideal exemplification of the fundamental impulse to inspire to the construction of evermore ambitious buildings.

South transept, Cathedral of SS Gervase et Protase c. 1180–1190, Soissons, France

One of the most visible formal characteristics of Gothic architecture is its precise graphic quality, its linearity and its subdivision of internal surfaces by means of cornices and shafts. The ribs of the vaults, which are continued down the walls all the way down to the ground plane, create cellular spaces and produce a multiple visual effect. A passage runs through the walls of the south transept at Soissons (triforia and galleries at window level), where the rear wall remains visible and seems be divided in two: this doubling effect emphasises the impression of ephemerality of the walls, creating an airy and translucent grille.

Since the 19th century, Gothic architecture has been classified by the critics according to the use of typical features: pointed arches, ogival ribs supporting the vaulting, clustered piers, tracery in the windows — especially in the rose windows — and flying buttresses on the exterior. Pointed arches, whether lancet or ogival, are created by the intersection of two arcs of a circle that meet at the apex. This is not a Gothic invention, but rather oriental in origin and was introduced in the West via Islamic buildings in Spain and Sicily. The novelty lies in the conscious and widespread use that Gothic architecture makes of the pointed arch. This preference was due to its greater structural efficiency compared with the round arch used in Romanesque architecture. This efficiency exists because, for a given quantity of light and weight, the pointed arch and vault impose a lower horizontal thrust on the vertical supports. Thus, it is possible to rib-vault any kind of floor plan. The extreme nature of Gothic cross vaults means that the buttresses — vertical structural elements used to strengthen the structure by absorbing the load it carries — are placed on the exterior of the building. Buttresses are often strengthened by pinnacle extensions. These have an important role in relieving the outer walls of their load-bearing function so that they can be replaced by large surfaces of coloured stained glass that reflect daubs of coloured light into the space and transform the interior of the building as the quality of light changes through the day. The buttresses are usually formed as flying buttresses (a quarter circle) to absorb and distribute the lateral thrusts of the upper parts of the building. By virtue of the great variety in the way in which these features can be combined, we can identify regional or national chracteristics of Gothic architecture and distinguish various stages in their evolution.

The structural and the figurative design of Gothic architecture meant that walls planes were dispensed with in favour of pillars, thereby evolving a skeletal system — i.e. a structural system within which there is a strict interaction of thrust and counterthrust that allowed the medieval architects to achieve great virtuosity with a skeleton wall that is both slender and elegant. Furthermore, Gothic architecture is typified by the pronounced verticality of the load-bearing structures achieved by the consistent use of pointed rib-vaulting and clustered piers.

The Gothic system pinpoints the forces acting within the structure, their position, direction and level of strain (thrust of the vaulting, weight of the roof and of vertical wall mass) for the purpose of setting up a structural framework that ensures the stability of the building and distributes the forces along pre-determined channels. Hence the clarity of framework that Gothic buildings have — in a state of distributed tension where the loads are rigidly localised.

The façades

Thanks to the use of features such as towers, spires, cusps and pinnacles, Gothic cathedrals express the same characteristic verticality on the exterior as they do on the interior. The twin-towered elevations of the northern French Gothic ('harmonic') are among the greatest achievements of medieval architecture. The employment of corner and lateral buttresses allowed for ever-wider openings, while the division into equal storeys corresponding to those

Façade of Wells Cathedral, 1230–1240, England

The most superb example of a screen façade among all the English cathedrals is undoubtedly that of Wells Cathedral. Here the towers are positioned on the sides and projecting buttresses articulate the building vertically. Rows of blind arcades superimposed above one another house the sculptures, which extend over the entire façade and illustrate the story of Salvation. In the passages, behind concealed openings there are spaces for the choir and orchestra.

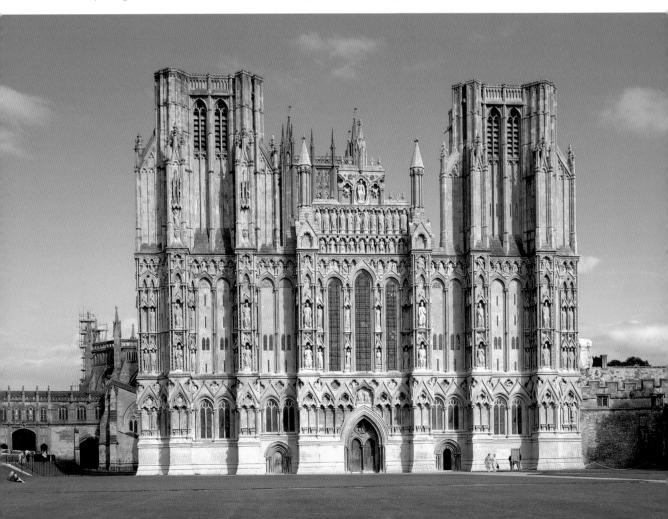

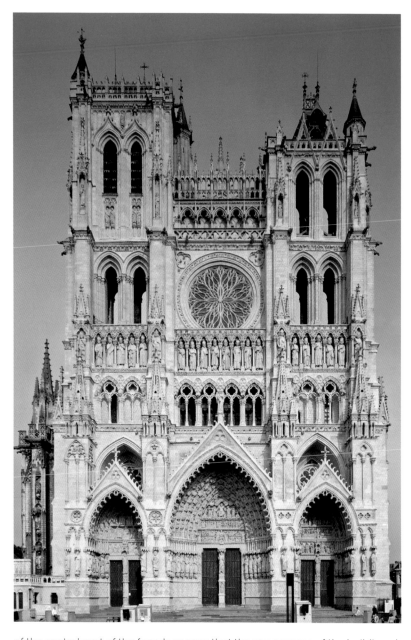

Robert de Luzarches, façade, Notre-Dame Cathedral, 1220, Amiens, France

The façade of Amiens is flanked by two towers which follow the dictates of the 'harmonious façade' — already explored in Anglo-Norman architecture. The façade is built in a tripartite configuration around the central rose window, which forms a seminal part of the composition, symbol of the sun (Christ) and of the rose (Mary), that ensures that the light shines into the building throughout the day until sunset. In accordance with the quest for reducing the weight of the structure, the architect has noticeably reduced the thickness of the masonry, stabilising the towers with enormous projecting buttresses into which the apertures of the side doors are inserted.

of the central part of the façade means that the appearance of the buildings became more and more unified. This unifying aspect was also achieved thanks to the rose windows — the great circular windows with decorated coloured glass intended as a generative feature of the composition and organisational element of the internal lighting — as well as the external arcades, which echoed the structure of the nave. Gothic buildings across the English Channel developed the 'screen façade', a western elevation which effectively hid the longitudinal body of the cathedral. The rejection of the French twin-towered façade composition in favour of a mainly horizontal façade composition is clearly illustrated by the three English churches: Peterborough (1201), Wells (1175–1490) and Salisbury (1220–1266).

The towers are either repositioned to the side elevations or project behind the façade wall, while the entry doorways assume no special significance and are often even obscured in the base as the main entrance is shifted to the northern elevation. Façades, which are aligned with the internal structures are especially rich in effects of chiaroscuro, thanks to the articulation by registers positioned above the small arcades intended to house the sculptural adornment. One needs to keep in mind that the cathedral has a dynamic relationship with the urban space in which it is situated. Initially, Gothic buildings did not adjoin large, open spaces but rather constricted, narrow access roads, whose obstructed views increased the effect of wonder at the unexpected appearance of the towers, belfries and spires standing tall against the sky, thrusting through the horizontal line of low medieval housing.

Architecture and ornament

During the Gothic period, sculpture had a far more organic relationship with architecture than in the Romanesque period. In Gothic architecture sculptural decoration extends across almost the entire building — an exuberant plethora of sculpture that follows the architectural design trends, particularly in the late Middle Ages. Symbols and allegories are used in the iconography of all the sculptures adorning the building, but are concentrated over the entrances, thus transforming the entrances to seem like the entrance to the kingdom of heaven with the intricate portrayal of the Last Judgment and the symbolic identification of the doorway with Christ himself (*ianua coeli* — gate of heaven), whose figure is carved on the tympanum, or trumeau — the pillar that divides the entrance in order to relieve the architrave.

It is nigh impossible to document the vast wealth of sculptures that decorate cathedrals all around Europe. The search to find harmonious forms and to find a balance between an ideal reality and human sensibility that characterises the 'classics' would soon deteriorate in favour of a gradually increasing naturalism; a quest for harmony, expressiveness and formal elegance. During the first half of the 13th century a great wealth of French Gothic sculpture extend-

Gargoyles of Notre-Dame Cathedral, 12–13th centuries, Paris, France

Typical of Gothic architecture, the gargoyles of Notre-Dame — sculptural waterspouts projecting from the eaves to drain rainwater — bear the features of monsters culled from medieval bestiaries.

Naumburg Master, Ekkehard and Uta, sculptures in Naumburg Cathedral, 1249, Germany

Religious architecture is not unaffected by courtly aspects; political intentions could have an influence on the choice of the ornamentation.
This is the case with the life-sized statues representing the founders of the earlier cathedral of Naumburg (11th century), which are distinguished by their aristocratic manner. Contemporary attire lends the sculptures a lifelike appearance: Margrave Ekkehard rests his hand on the hilt of his sword to remind us of his sovereign status, while his wife, Uta, expresses a haughty aloofness.

ed into German-speaking territories, like Bamberg, Naumburg and Magdeburg, in the large cathedrals founded by the military or medical orders, which evolved into monumental forms. As with architecture however, in Italy, architectural sculpture developed and changed in different periods according to fashions and trends. Though in the sculptures of Benedetto Antelami there are signs of an awareness of French sculpture from the Île-de-France. Nourished by classical ideas, the Gothic spirit manifested itself in the marvellous churches of Nicola and Giovanni Pisano, whilst architects like Arnolfo di Cambio chose a different avenue where classical ideals prevailed.

The windows

Coloured stained glass windows are one of the most important components of Gothic architecture creating radiant, glowing interiors which vary according to the intensity of the light. The development of stained glass windows

The King's Portal, Cathedral of Notre-Dame, c. 1145–1155, Chartres, France

A masterpiece of early Gothic sculpture can be seen in the ensemble of the three western portals of Chartres Cathedral, where the holy figures take the form of the columns: these caryatids are carved from the same quarried stone as the columns of the embrasure.

Doorways of this kind already existed in Romanesque pilgrim churches, but were first found in complete form in the (now destroyed) portals of Saint-Denis, becoming a permanent feature of Gothic buildings during the course of the 12th century.

The three western portals of Chartres Cathedral are linked either by architraves of the same height or by the unbroken line of capitals on which various episodes of Christ's life are depicted.

On the following pages
Salisbury Cathedral, 1220–1266, England

was the result of a long and complex process requiring highly skilled labour. The various stages of the work comprised producing the glass, blowing the panes, cutting them to fit prepared designs, assembling the picture on the panels, making them up with lead cames and installing them in the windows with metallic frames. The iconography typical of the coloured glass windows includes the sacred figures of the Virgin, Christ, the apostles and prophets, advancing to more complex compositions drawn from the Scriptures and the lives of saints. There was also a great range of people from every social echelon who commissioned these precious windows; kings down to people from humble backgrounds. Between the 12th and 13th centuries the range of subjects was regulated: stories from Old and New Testaments and saints' lives with narrative content, which require careful reading, usually appear on the lowest area of the windows, while iconic representations appear on the upper areas. The theological conception of the cathedral as a transposition of Heavenly Jerusalem to Earth — a translucent structure of light and mystical space where one can immerse oneself — has ensured that Gothic windows have come to be regarded as 'coloured walls' or 'bejewelled walls', mystical and sensory. Furthermore, recent writers, drawing attention to the iconographical breadth of the stained glass windows have interpreted the light shining through the windows as being symbolic of the light on the journey believers must tread to reach Paradise.

opposite page
Pierre de Montreuil, Sainte-Chapelle, 1241–1248, Paris

The technical possibilities of the skeleton framework of Gothic architecture are taken to extremes in the Sainte-Chapelle: beneath the ogival vaulting and between the slender piers of clustered shafts the wall disappears, to be replaced by an almost continuous sheet of glass. Coupled with the quality of the architectural space is the rich ornamentation; the use of colour and a flood of light — sparkling and multi-coloured — that streams through the tracery of the huge stained glass windows. With its translucent walls, Sainte-Chapelle is a kind of monumental stone reliquary, which was built to contain the crown of thorns and relics of the Crucifixion that Louis IX had brought to France. The sacred and royal function of the church is clearly illustrated in the decoration of the windows: stained glass adorned with Bible scenes, while the cornices bear the heraldic emblem of the *fleur de lys*.

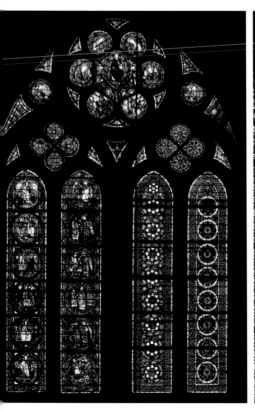 

Upper windows of the Basilica of St Francis, mid-13th century, Assisi, Italy (left)
Windows illustrating the life of St Stephen, 1210–1215, Ambulatory, Bourges Cathedral, France (right)

The lives of locally venerated saints — whose good deeds are inscribed in hagiographic texts crammed full of miracles and wonders — were translated into images by master glass blowers following specifications from theologians. The idea being to stir the imaginations of the faithful, most of whom were illiterate.

ORIGINS OF GOTHIC ARCHITECTURE: THE ÎLE-DE-FRANCE

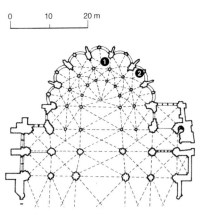

Choir ambulatory and floor plan, Abbey of Saint-Denis, 1144, France

Between 1140 and 1144, Abbot Suger initiated the rebuilding of the church of Saint-Denis in order to house the relics of St Denys and the remains of the kings of France. The renovation created the opportunity for radical innovation: a double ambulatory (1) around the end of the choir, with radial, rib-vaulted chapels (2). This represents the first structural plan, characterised by the distribution of loads and gravitational thrusts on to separate, slender supports. The innovation lay in the dissolution of the walls and their replacement with stained glass windows.

Convention among historians puts the origin of the Gothic structural system as dating from the rebuilding of the church of Saint-Denis near Paris in around 1140. The church was the burial chapel of the Capetian dynasty.

The newly built choir, consecrated in 1144, was designed to accommodate a steady flow of pilgrims, but was also an early recognition of the potential spaciousness of the new architecture. The effect of its generous dimensions and its vertical height was also due to the conscious use of light. Thereafter, between 1140 and 1190, the architecture of the Royal Domain discovered structural solutions that were to be particular to Gothic architecture. Finding appropriate solutions to the challenges of creating the soaring heights of Gothic churches took half a century of intense experimentation. The structural solutions found accentuated the vertical articulation of the church whilst simultaneously creating a far greater range of forms and effects of transparency and luminosity in the internal space.

The common objective was to extend the height of the building as far as possible. This was translated into a four-level elevation, while the continuity between nave, transept and choir permitted the creation of elegant interiors. The most important early examples are to be found in Noyon, Laon and Paris. During the late 1100s, the stonemasons' yards at Laon and Paris experimented with, and perfected, several technical innovations: Notre-Dame Cathedral counterbalances the thrust of the nave vault with flying buttresses, while Laon Cathedral translates the reduction of the walls as a stripping back of the exterior walls. Experiments like these were to influence the flying buttresses of Chartres Cathedral.

Façade of the Cathedral of Notre-Dame, c. 1190, Laon, France

Thanks to the subdivision of the west elevation into three separate sections, created by shifting the doorways forward with the insertion of deep porticos whilst shifting the towers backwards, the 'harmonic façade' of Laon gained a new spaciousness, accentuated by the colossal dimensions of the openings and the enormous central rose window; focus of the whole composition. This configuration represents a special achievement for Gothic architecture as, for the first time, the twin-towered façade was connected to the internal space from the onset and was no longer a separate, independent structure.

CISTERCIAN ARCHITECTURE

With the adoption of a monastic code that was based on returning to the simplicity of the past, Bernard of Clairvaux was instrumental in promoting a genre of architecture that reflected this search for asceticism and clarity. Right from the onset, the agenda of Cistercian architecture was imbued by a religious spirit staunchly opposed to the enormous scale and sumptuous architectural decoration of buildings like at Cluny and Saint-Denis. Great frugality in the use of resources that were imposed resulted in a spartan but functional monumentality. The Cistercian order was one of the forerunners in adopting the pointed-arch. However, this did not always produce the clear, rigorous subdivision of space typical of Gothic cathedrals. In fact Cistercian architecture of the 12th century has even been called 'reduced Gothic', i.e. reduced to technical processes and to a new spatial definition that replaced decorative forms.

Only subsequent to the construction of the new apse at Pontigny (1185) did Cistercian architects begin to move away from their primitive simplicity, drawing closer to the ornate style of the great cathedrals. From 1185 onwards, the adherence of Cistercian architecture to Gothic precepts gained momentum — if with different forms and typologies. Cistercian architects renounced complex typologies and, at least initially, crossing towers, west fronts and belfries, which were prohibited. The expansion of the order was striking; during the second half of the 12th century the 'simplified' Gothic of the Cistercians was exported abroad, where the call to the renewed Gothic architecture had been absent, for instance: the French Midi, Spain, Italy, England, the German Empire, as well as Poland and Hungary.

Cistercian Abbey of Notre-Dame, Final third of 12th century, Pontigny, France

Of the five founding abbeys which once constituted the Cistercian order — along with Cîteaux, Clairvaux, Morimond and La Ferté — Pontigny is the only one which survives to the present day despite the French Revolution and the havoc it wrought. In the second half of the 12th century, the abbey was a construction site, which was truly experimental. Insofar as, shortly after completion of the church, the choir which had only been built a few years earlier was demolished to make way for a new structure for the monks (who had increased in number in the meantime) to celebrate daily mass. The exact date the choir was built is unknown, but stylistic elements suggest that it was built towards the end of the 12th century. The splendid articulation of the flying buttresses gives the interior an opulence and magnificence unusual in the churches of the Order, where every excess was expressly forbidden.

Cistercian Abbey of Rievaulx, founded in 1132, Yorkshire, England

At a very early date, in the 1130s, the Cistercians arrived in England and subsequently built a great number of conventional churches there. Almost all of these churches lie in ruins today. The Rievaulx Abbey is clearly French in origin as can be seen in the triple elevation, which is subdivided by horizontal cornices associated with strongly articulated walls. It has arcading featuring pointed arches with complex mouldings supported by clustered piers.

Washbasin, Poblet Monastery, 1151, Spain

The second half of the 12th century in Spain saw a great number of Cistercian orders established. The priests and monks introduced the first elements of French Gothic to Spain, including rib-vaulting. However, despite the use of pointed arches and ribbed vaults, as in the Poblet wash-basin, the layout remained traditional and the mass of the volumes produces an effect more typical of previous Romanesque churches.

EARLY ENGLISH: THE FIRST ENGLISH GOTHIC ARCHITECTURE

Towards the end of the 12th century in England, there were a few buildings which indicated great originality in interpreting French prototypes. These buildings had triple-storey elevations structured as longitudinal sections placed above the entire length of the nave without any vertical connection. This prefigured the tendency towards a horizontal format, which would typify English Gothic architecture. After the loss of territories on the Continent in 1204, English masons distanced themselves further and stressed their independence from French examples. The creative quest of English masons bypassed the rigorously logical structure of transalpine architecture in favour of particular decorative effects, which arose from a taste for the unique and for precious materials.

Furthermore, English churches did not adopt spatial plans that were characterised by rare perspective rhythms such as the most convincing examples at Bourges. The Anglo-Norman building technique of the 'thick wall' of great depth was retained. English cathedrals remained longitudinal due to the accentuated horizontality of the arcades, matronea and galleries, while the verticality of the pillars was reduced.

However, some peripheral areas illustrate experimentation with original solutions like the effects of increasing spatial volume or else the detail of the window tracery. Simultaneous to this, the first screen façades appear as a clear indication of the rejection of the French twin-towered façades in favour of a predominantly horizontal typology.

opposite page
Ground plan and cross-section of Lincoln Cathedral, begun 1192, England

Rebuilt after a destructive earthquake in 1185, which only spared the west front, Lincoln Cathedral has a Latin-cross floor plan with a nave and two side aisles plus a double transept (1), a rectangular choir and ambulatory (2) and a tripartite elevation, wide arches (3), a triforium (4) almost the size of a gallery and clerestory lights (5) with windows screened by internal arches. Lincoln Cathedral expresses the character of extreme adornment typical of English Gothic architecture. This was also adopted in St Hugh's Choir, an asymmetrical vaulting scheme, rendered more complex by the insertion of supplementary ribbing: the 'crazy vaulting', which was an early indication of various Late Gothic solutions, is rendered possible by the use of massive, unbroken walls; the result being a pattern, more decorative than structural.

Detail of St Hugh's Choir, Lincoln Cathedral, 1192–1205, England

An eccentric solution to a problem, which occurred in the first phase of construction at Lincoln cathedral, can be seen in the lower area of the aisles of St Hugh's Choir as well as in the east transept: a double series of staggered arcades placed one in front of the other. The lower arcade at the rear gives an illusion of greater depth and is reminiscent of the typically English penchant for partition walls and rich sculptural decoration.

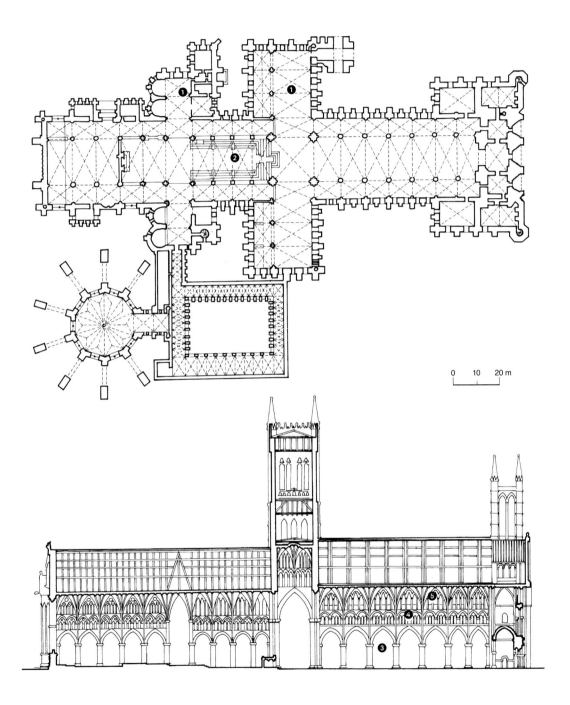

THE MASTERPIECE
CANTERBURY CATHEDRAL

In 1174, a raging inferno almost completely destroyed the east end of Canterbury cathedral. Shortly thereafter English and French master builders were summoned to put forward their proposals for the reconstruction of the damaged sections. French master mason, William of Sens, suggested rebuilding the choir in a new form, responding to the need to enlarge this part of the building, as it had become a place of ever-growing pilgrimage after the martyrdom, and canonisation of Archbishop Thomas Becket in 1170. The contemporary chronicle by the monk, Gervase of Canterbury, not only acknowledges the fame that architects of the Île-de-France enjoyed at that time, confirming their activity out-

side their country of origin. Moreover, the monk's chronicle also illustrates how early on the new Gothic language of architecture was accepted in England. Of all cathedrals in England, Canterbury is the one cathedral that has the greatest affinity with continental architecture. Canterbury Cathedral is brimming with innovations. Sens invented a new concept of 'thick wall' in the triforium and clerestory, increasing the linear effect through the use of small, dark Purbeck marble shafts that contrast dramatically with the light hue of the limestone of the structural elements. Sens gives a decorative impression quite foreign to French practice that would become an integrated feature of English Gothic.

Floor plan, Canterbury Cathedral, 1390–1410, England

The ground floor plan of Canterbury Cathedral portrays an elongated church with two transepts (3): Trinity Chapel (1) opens beyond the high altar and terminates with an axial chapel called the Crown of Becket (2). Both chapels are dedicated to the cult of the saint. The coffin rests in the chapel, while the Crown has the reliquary containing the saint's head.

Choir of Canterbury Cathedral, post 1174, England

The Canterbury Cathedral choir was built in the early years of Early English Gothic by William the Englishman, deputy to his French colleague, William of Sens, who returned to his homeland, France, in 1178. The choir reworks some elements from Saint-Denis, adopting the ambulatory in a wholly exceptional manner for English architecture; while the curves of the walls demarkate it as a unique phenomenon in all medieval architecture. Although created in special circumstances — the cult of Thomas Becket and the consequent influx of pilgrims — Cantebury Cathedral choir influenced many Early English Gothic choirs and was thought to be an efficient way of enclosing the relics of the saints.

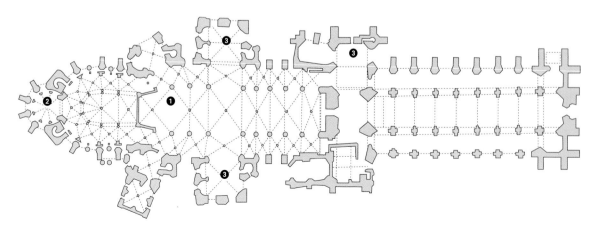

HIGH GOTHIC

The architectural evolution of cathedrals from Early to Late Gothic went hand in hand with an ever-greater luminosity and the associated replacement of solid walls by huge tracts of stunning stained glass. The flying buttresses, which permitted this process, spread rapidly, developing into elaborate and complex structural schemes. To achieve this end, evermore massive buttresses were constructed, surmounted by tabernacles and spires, which fundamentally altered the external appearance of the building, breaking up the volumes into a kind of kaleidoscope of forms. Equally important were the modifications of the interior, as the use of flying buttresses allowed increases in height up to the maximum technically possible. The layout of the nave now reached its mature form, articulated in a large tripartite elevation by eliminating the women's gallery.

It was at the two great construction sites of Bourges and Chartres that the potential for innovation inherent in this change was used to achieve a new monumental appearance, in a quest for balance and harmony between the parts and the whole. This aspiration was pursued through the use of simple, rhythmic relationships, imbued with the Neo-Platonism and Augustinianism of the clients. Such trends justify the use of the term High Gothic to describe the cathedrals of Chartres, Bourges, Rheims and Amiens and, more generally, the experimentation of the first three decades of the 13th century. The monumental idea of the great cathedrals was also an expression of the power of the Capetian monarchy under Philip II Augustus, while the spread of Gothic forms throughout Europe would be linked to the growing influence of French politics and culture during the 13th century.

Choir of the Jacobin church, begun 1233, Toulouse, France

At the same time, the growth of towns represented the transition from the immobility and isolation of the countryside to the mobility and flexibility of modern culture. At first, towns bore the imprint of medieval social groupings — compared with rural communities, towns were distinguished by their markets and their administrative autonomy, coupled with the fact that they constituted an independent judicial district. Even the smallest towns were fortified, due to the high levels of insecurity. A fortified wall was added to the existing ramparts and ditches, with towers and the minimum number of gateways, which were locked at night and guarded during the daytime. This was not solely a matter of defence; fortified towns were intended to overtake territorial control of other lands. In France, the first planned fortified cities were established during the reigns of Louis VII and Louis IX with the task of supporting their policy of expansion. The south witnessed a proliferation of 'refuge villages' — their urban structure was determined by topographical conditions and political necessity. Thus, the high, fortified town is generally situated on the crest of a hill from where it dominates the surrounding territory, as in the case of Carcassonne, or else the town is surrounded by river or water, like Aigues-Mortes in the Camargue, or even by the seawater, like Saint-Malo in Brittany or Caernarvon in Wales.

Saint-Malo, 12th–18th century, France

Founded in the 12th century on a rocky islet, with its historic centre entirely surrounded by ramparts, Saint-Malo was an independent maritime city and lair of pirates in the pay of the king.
The walls of the city were built in the 12th century and were continually extended up until the 18th century. The Grande-Porte was built in the 15th century to defend the port.

Apse of St Stephen's Cathedral, 1195–1214, Bourges, France

In the great stonemasons' yard of Bourges, experiments were carried out to test the possibility of developing Gothic architecture in order to give it a monumental appearance by means of slender, vertical buttresses and light, flying buttresses.

The urban monastery

In the heart of the new medieval urban culture, the mendicant orders (Augustinians, Dominicans, Franciscans) became spokespeople for the more restless and reforming elements, who were opposed to the opulence and lavishness of those closely linked to the papacy or to the Empire and to the dissolute, debauched lifestyle that towns fostered. The urban monastery thus appeared in places where the wealth of the new bourgeoisie was woven into the texture of urban life, developing on an L-shaped plan where church and monastic accommodation overlooked a square — a place for both encounters and preaching. From the last three decades of the 13th century, the steady growth of the mendicant movement caused a radical change in building policy that resulted in the construction of very large buildings.

The choice of typology was often determined by the churches with an aisleless nave, which permitted simplicity of construction to be combined with the huge scale necessary to accommodate large congregations into a space with no obstacles to listening to the sermon. These churches were economic to build and were relatively quick to be constructed, thus transforming the display of poverty into an expression and symbol of grandeur. Expressive ecumenical buildings appeared in great numbers in France and in Italy. The Dominican order was founded in Toulouse in 1215 to combat heresy. In the Po Valley, the style of the order was grafted on to local Cistercian traditions, resulting in the simplification of the buildings. While in the central regions of the peninsula, where new orders sprung up and developed, the ascetic ideal of renouncing excess was translated into three dimensions by a nave and high, bare walls punctured with large windows: a stark, bleak space perhaps, but huge, imposing and solemn.

left
Nave of Notre-Dame cathedral, begun 1220, Amiens, France

Notre-Dame is the largest of the French cathedrals. Its structure harmoniously adheres to the dictates of High Gothic, interpreted in grandiose, monumental forms. In fact, the cathedral represents a step forward in the enhancement of Gothic scale. The builders of Amiens, like those of Chartres and Bourges, experimented with the cantoned pier — a pillar with four columns adjoined to it, which flow uninterruptedly up to the vault, accentuating the verticality.

below
Apsidal view of the Cathedral of St Etienne, begun 1215, Auxerre, France

A masterpiece of Burgundian Gothic, this cathedral is a regional variant of High Gothic which does not yield to the gigantism of the great cathedrals, rather limiting the height of the building.
The exterior, which features a single tower on the façade and simple flying arches around the choir, matches the simplicity of the internal space.

Rayonnant Gothic

Techniques investigated at Rheims and Amiens predicted the beginning of a divergence of taste that has been given the name *rayonnant* (radiant), based on the radial design of the tracery in the great rose windows. Monumentality, previously expressed in heavy bulk, was abandoned in favour of fragility that reduced forms to a pure network of lines both two and three-dimensional. However, without radically transforming the structure of the Gothic church, which continued to use the Chartres model both in ground floor plan and in elevation. Verticality was taken to its absolute limit, all elements became more slender and more linear, without depth in the treatment of surfaces and visually weightless. Saint Denis Church was once more in the vanguard of change with the construction of a new type of pillar, which made up from a dense cluster of shafts, thus altering the design of the nave into a pattern of purely graphic lines. Moreover, the builders concentrated on designing a stone shell, which structured and adorned the window lights, gradually becoming more and more elaborate. Externally, they forewent scale in favour of fuller and more balanced proportions. The incredible spread of the Rayonnant methodology sprang from the prestige of the Capetian monarchy and perhaps also from an ideological desire, on the part of the builders, to adhere to the preordained style of a great Christian state. The advance of Rayonnant Gothic was interrupted around 1340 due to the recurrent blight of the plague and the dark period of the Hundred Years' War. In addition, the change of dynasty to the house of Valois, who came to the throne in 1328, brought about a progressive desacralisation of the figure of the king and rekindled feudal particularism, causing a slowdown in religious building whilst at the same time stimulating military, civil and royal architecture.

above
Arnolfo di Cambio, interior of the basilica of Santa Croce, begun 1295, Florence

In Tuscany the idea of a unified space pervaded with diffuse light was achieved thanks to the great height of the aisles. This concept was to find its purest expression in the Franciscan church of Santa Croce in Florence. In this church, Arnolfo di Cambio conceived a basilica that responded to the requirements of reformed Gothic — simplicity and lack of ornament. The structural simplicity is evident in the T-shaped floor plan, stripped of complex presbyterial features.

opposite page
Jacobin church, begun 1233, Toulouse, France

Of the mendicant churches of southern France, it is the Jacobin church in Toulouse which offers an enormous rectangular space. The row of massive cylindrical pillars, the high, lofty space and the broad windows surrounding the building, create an architectural genre that typifies the south of France.

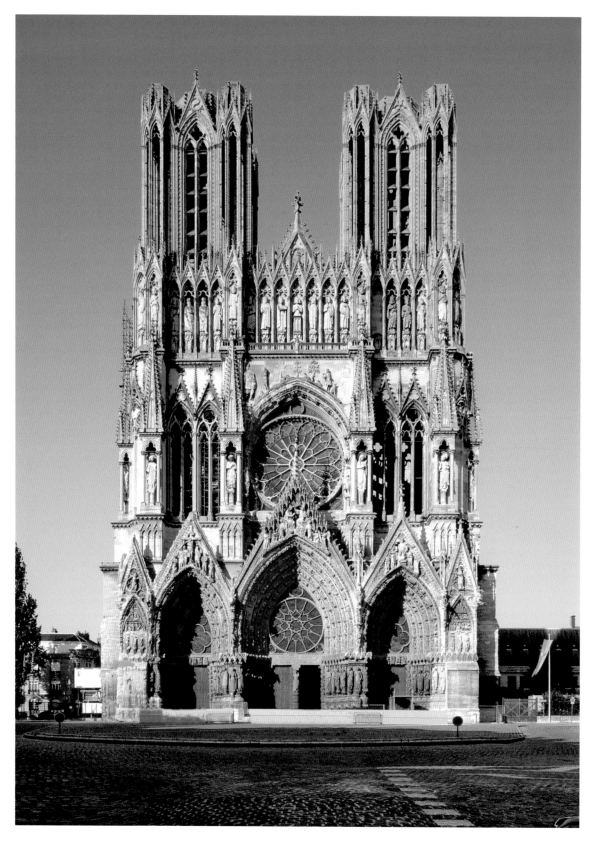

opposite page
Bernard de Soissons, façade of the Cathedral of Notre-Dame, c. 1250 Rheims, France

The façade of Rheims presents a continuous sequence of thin, slender triangular *wimperg* gables above the three, deeply splayed portals which are counterbalanced by the clever transformation of the tympanum into windows that allow light to radiate into the entrance area.

The front elevation is divided into three horizontal bands, as in the cathedral in Paris, but the verticality is more accentuated, as every element is pointed and slender. The façade integrates previous solutions, but is original in the combination of contrasting forms and in the way they are configured — the centrality of the rose window contrasts with the narrow lateral apertures with their fine tracery.

above left
Crossing of the abbatial Church of Saint Denis, begun 1231, France

It is not surprising that one of the first buildings to be built in the new Gothic style should be St Denis, rebuilt from 1231 onwards, at the behest of Eudes de Clément, in order to strengthen the church's importance as a royal burial place. The architect respected the older sections of Suger's choir, but in the other areas of the church he adopted a revolutionary clustered pier enclosed with shafts which soar uninterrupted from floor to vault and which provide an innovative layout for the upper section of the nave — an elegant triforium lit by set-back windows, a clerestory with beautiful lanceolate windows and splendid rose windows in the transept that articulate the space.

above right
Chapel of the Castle of Saint-Germain-en-Laye, begun 1238, France

The new architectural style of Saint Denis was applied in a deliberately spectacular way in the little royal chapel built by Louis IX. As in the abbey church, sacred architecture had reached an unsurpassed excellence and compositional logic, defining a process of standardisation that lasted more than 150 years.

next double page
View of León Cathedral from the south-east, c. 1225, León, Spain

THE CHARTRES MODEL

The Cathedral of Notre-Dame at Chartres, one of the most significant Marian sanctuaries of France, represented the prototype of a true Gothic cathedral. Its characteristic features are length, a nave-and-two-aisled floor plan, a tripartite elevation (arcade, triforium, clerestory), followed by a short transept and terminating in a deep presbytery with an ambulatory and radial chapels. The sumptuous reconstruction of the building followed almost immediately with the fire of 1194, which spared only the crypt of the previous church and the west façade with its doorways and two towers. The construction of the choir in about 1221 completed the reconstruction. The rectangular bays are covered by quadripartite ribbed vaults that rest on supports. From this arrangement flows a dynamic, continuous rhythm that enhances the verticality by means of the innovative cantoned pier, used in Chartres for the first time. The Chartres formula — i.e. the elimination of the women's gallery (made possible by the use of external flying buttresses to strengthen the vaulting), the enlarging of the clerestory, the rectangular bays, the quadripartite vault (with four panels) and the cantoned pier — was an immediate success. In a simple, clear way, it fulfilled the need for streamlining the building process and lent the cathedral rare grandeur. In the shadow of this great building site, 'intellectual thinkers', like Theodoric of Chartres and William of Conches, would further define the Gothic aesthetic, through which the *anima mundi*, the 'living energy of creation', is reflected — both in the articulated tension of the architectural structure and in the varied and unusual repertory of sculptural adornment.

opposite page
West front of Chartres Cathedral, pre-1194, France

Nave and detail of Chartres Cathedral, c. 1194–1221, France

Chartres is a classical building in its proportions, with the arches and the clerestory at similar heights. Furthermore, the new requirements for the congregation to be able to see the altar during celebration of the Eucharist required a new arrangement of the choir.

THE TERRITORIES OF THE GERMAN EMPIRE

Exterior and floor plan of the Liebfrauenkirche, 1235–1260, Trier, Germany

The influence of French architecture in the Liebfrauenkirche is shown in the adoption of the cantoned pier (1) and Rheims-type windows. It is an unusual church, which reinterprets French models with great flair, freely superimposing volumes vertically onto one another in a pyramidal effect, without any need for flying buttresses thanks to the thickness of the walls. The church is built on the remains of an old centrally planned church and adheres to its Greek cross layout (with the exception of the

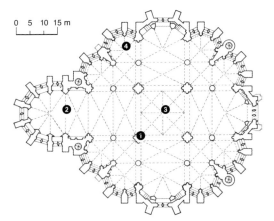

The structural and linguistic concepts of Gothic architecture were slow to extend into German-speaking areas. For a large part of the 13th century, buildings in the heart of the Empire continued to be built primarily in the traditional manner — faithful to massive proportions and 'thick wall' techniques. German builders harboured a taste for overabundant external architectural ornamentation with no rhythmic articulation of volumes by the use of vertical or flying buttresses. The eclipse of imperial authority after the death of Hohenstaufen emperor, Henry VI, and the Italian policies of Frederick II led to artistic fragmentation, so that the response to the solutions developed in the various French cathedrals were altered or were smothered by conservative forces. However, at the start of the 13th century, resistance tended to gradually fade away in favour of adopting the spatial concept of French Gothic — a choice which was manifest, above all, in the structure of the supports. At the beginning of the 14th century Strasbourg and Cologne remained the biggest construction sites in the Empire, some important buildings there confirm the maturity achieved by German Gothic and its early transition to Late Gothic forms.

extension of the polygonal east choir), (2) the crossing tower(3) obscured on the outside by the introduction of radial chapels (4) as if to outline a bloom with twelve petals.

**opposite page
Choir of the cathedral, late 13th century, Limburg an der Lahn, Germany**

The diocese of Trier was a metropolitan centre near French territory and was a kind of threshold for the Gothic style to enter Germany. The collegiate church of Limburg an der Lahn, part of the Trier diocese, is characterised by clustered piers surmounted by a polygonal cupola in its markedly vertical choir.

THE MASTERPIECE
STRASBOURG CATHEDRAL

left
**Michele da Friburgo, detail of
the design for the west front
of Strasbourg Cathedral, mid-
14th century, Musée de l'Œuvre
Notre-Dame, Strasbourg, France**

A number of scale drawings on parchment analysing different design solutions put forward for the great central rose window and its carved ornamentation reflect the rigorous amount of work on the cathedral façade. The remarkable size of the drawings — the drawings for the whole façade measure 410 x 82.5 cm — and the use of colour, like a miniature painting, suggest that they were intended to be presented to the clients.

**Erwin von Steinbach, rose window
(above) and façade (opposite page)
of Strasbourg Cathedral, begun
1275, Strasbourg, France**

The use of soft, red sandstone is what feasibly made the extraordinary virtuosity of the façade at all possible. 'Harp tracery' — i.e. staggering various elements over several layers against the rear wall — is taken to its ultimate extreme here. The huge, magnificent rose window in the centre of the façade is recessed into the same surface as the tracery.

The events surrounding the construction of Strasbourg Cathedral are undeniable proof of the progressive evolution of Gothic solutions from the initial hostile attitude among builders in the Rhine area, to the eventual embrace of the new forms. The rebuilding of the Ottonian Cathedral began with the transept in around 1176 and continued until 1210 and again, later, with the construction of the choir between 1220 and 1225 and north façade of the transept in a primarily Late Romanesque style. There was a change of course with the arrival in the masons' yard of a French architect commissioned with rebuilding the southern façade, where he employed a cylindrical pillar with eight shafts and raised the height of the walls, piercing them with large windows similar to those at Chartres.

These innovations met with immediate success and, from that moment onwards, the Strasbourg masons' yard became one of the principal centres of the dissemination and development of Rayonnant Gothic, coinciding with the city's economic heyday and the civic authority taking charge of construction works.
The role that Strasbourg played for the Upper Rhine paralleled the role that Cologne played for the Lower Rhine. The old cathedral had become too small and out-dated to house the relics of the three Magi, an essential point from the viewpoint of imperial politics — hence the desire to build the ultimate 'perfect' cathedral.

THE MASTERPIECE
COLOGNE CATHEDRAL

Rayonnant Gothic forms spread quickly beyond French borders; the great trading cities, among them Cologne, were the first to welcome its arrival. The first move to rebuild the old Ottonian basilica dated from the second decade of the 13th century, but it was only after the fire of 1248 that the new construction actually progressed according to a previously devised plan of French provenance. It is probable that the client — Bishop Conrad of Hochstaden, a supporter of the anti-Swabian policies of Louis IX — wanted the great municipal masons' yard to reflect the formal elegance of contemporary Parisian constructions like Sainte-Chapelle. The construction works progressed very slowly. Consecrated in 1322, whilst still incomplete, work began on the façade in 1350. The cathedral would only be finished finally in the 19th century, though still according to the original plan. The resumption of High Gothic forms, developed at Amiens, is mainly evident in the arrangement of buttresses and in the very acute-angled *wimperg* gables above the openings, where the three-lobe motif, called a *dreistrahl*, can be seen.

The surface of the walls disappears almost completely behind a delicate pattern of highly decorated pinnacles, which restore unity to the complex volumetry of the building. The Cologne masons' yard, like that of Strasbourg, thus became one of the principal centres of the development of Rayonnant Gothic, where it is difficult — in contrast with most German masons' yards — to recognise the continuance of the German tradition.

Vault of the choir of Cologne Cathedral, 1248–1322, Germany

The proportions of Cologne Cathedral show a conspicuous vertical momentum and the huge windows allow an intense luminosity into the building. The 'modernity' of Cologne is regarded in its bright triforium like a delicate piece of filigree work. The vault shows the abandonment of the Chartres-model cantoned pier in favour of a Saint Denis-style clustered pier with shafts that rise uninterrupted to meet the ribs of the vault.

Façade of Cologne Cathedral, begun 1350, Germany

The west elevation of Cologne Cathedral, begun in 1350 and completed only in 1842–1880 according to the original design, is articulated by five massive buttresses each corresponding to the internal aisles. There are only three entrance doorways, as the exterior spaces are appropriated by great windows and two impressive towers.

Floor plan of Cologne Cathedral, begun 1248, Germany

The general plan layout of the building is similar to that of Amiens Cathedral, but with a few key differences: the longitudinal structure with its projecting transept has a nave and double aisles (1) rather than single aisles, a wide transept (2) a choir with a double ambulatory (3) and radial chapels (4). The presence of a deep westwork (5) (a kind of multi-storey atrium at the west end) shortens the nave, making the church almost central-plan — perhaps a reminder of local traditions, which were Carolingian in origin.

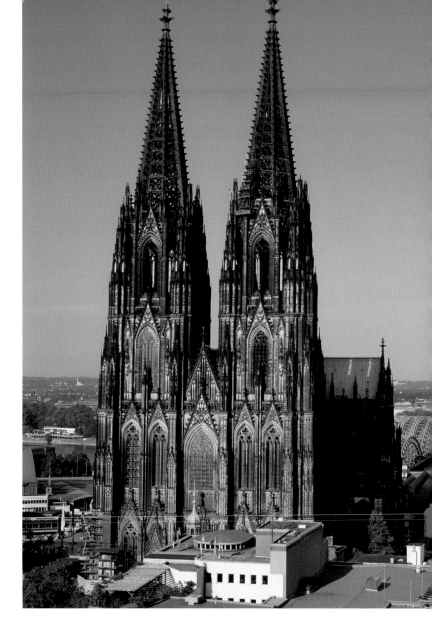

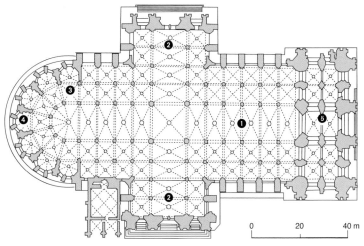

HANSEATIC CITIES AND THE BALTIC

In the north European region, which lacked stone quarries from which to extract construction materials, brick was the basic material of the Gothic style. In its monumental humility, the architecture suited the monotonous landscape. In these regions, the use of brick led to a completely individual style that, in the compactness of its forms, contrasted strongly with the extreme lightness sought in Gothic architecture. However, towards the end of the 13th century German architects succeeded in combining a new expression, which became familiar through the crucial Cistercian influence, with the use of this inexpensive material. The masonry creates a particular Gothic style coined *Backsteingotik* (Brick Gothic) by German scholars. This Brick Gothic style was not only utilised in individual buildings, whether sacred or secular, but also in real urban planning, culminating in the unique ring of brick ramparts built around the city of Neubrandenburg.

The structure of these Baltic buildings, from Lübeck to Chorin, Prenzlau to Stralsund, clearly indicates a desire for simplification compared with the Gothic architecture of the great cathedrals — a simplicity dictated, in part, by the material used, which led to the construction of large areas of wall surface and, in part, to the tendency to reject excessive relief or indentation. These buildings did not, however, exclude sumptuous architecture and exquisite detail effects.

opposite page
West façade of Chorin Abbey, late 13th — early 14th century, Brandenburg, Germany

The Cistercian abbey of Chorin is one of the highlights of 'Brick Gothic' in northern Germany — the tripartite west front rises above the roof ridge, culminating in gables. The use of blind arcades and tracery conceals the real height of the building and its internal structure.

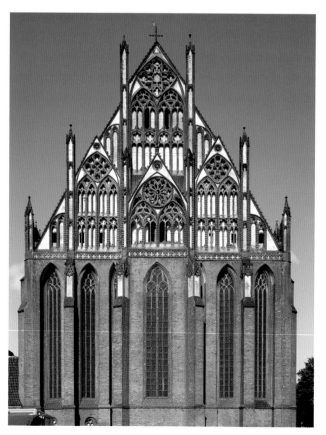

Marienkirche, begun 1325, Prenzlau, Germany

The beautiful east front of Prenzlau church provides a rich demonstration of the formal and picturesque qualities that can be achieved with brickwork. The church features a simple base and first storey articulated by high lanceolate windows between buttresses. A tympanum is grafted onto this, which is made of tracery, by means of a curtain wall of red and black brick applied to white-plastered masonry. The sumptuous articulation of Gothic elements on flat surfaces, made more complex by means of windows, triforia, gables and horizontal, vertical and diagonal directrices of vaulting, reaches its zenith in the Marienkirche.

THE MASTERPIECE
LÜBECK

Heiligen-Geist-Spital, begun 1280, Lübeck, Germany

This building, one of the oldest hospitals financed by local merchants, was intended to accommodate the sick and the infirm. The hospital has a T-shaped ground floor plan and a tripartite façade with buttresses whose slender pinnacles counterbalance the prevailing horizontality of the main body of the building. The three sections have triangular gables decorated with rows of blind two-pane mullioned windows and large window openings.

opposite page
Holstentor, 1464–1478, Lübeck, Germany

Built by local master, Heinrich Helmsted, the Holstentor — gateway to the old city — is the most famous city gateway in the medieval fortifications. The entry consists of two circular towers linked by a brick building that spans the gate. It is one of the most important examples of Baltic, Brick Gothic construction. It is a survivor of a series of defensive gates on the western side of the ring wall and expresses both the power and the pride of the city.

Lübeck was a key player in the economic organisation of the Baltic between the 13th and 15th centuries. It was also the most powerful city in the Hanseatic League, which was one of the most revolutionary commercial alliances of the late Middle Ages. The Hanseatic League (Hansa) was an alliance which linked the most important commercial centres of northern Europe and the Baltic. The league was entrusted with the colonisation and the spread of Christianity in the eastern territories with which it also forged economic ties. Surrounded by water, Lübeck built its huge towers as a symbol of its invincible power, flaunting its solemn image as a city-state. It had been a free city since 1226 and titular of a weak diocese (due to its lack of territorial power), it had a city council composed of wealthy merchants — an oligarchic predominance that reflected the urban structure perfectly. The reconstruction of the Marienkirche from 1277 was indeed due to the initiative of the merchants who provided the capital for the construction and managed the masons' yard. Furthermore — in order to demonstrate their elevated position in the social framework of the city — the scale and the position of the church rival that, and are more imposing than, the cathedral, which is situated in a peripheral area. Facing the market square is the *Rathaus* or town hall, which also served as a warehouse and commercial centre.

THE FRENCH MIDI

The architecture of the southern regions of France differs from that of the northern regions of the country. The provinces of Toulouse and Languedoc (extending from the Pyrenees to Avignon) were governed by local dynasties independent from the kingdom of France. Not until after the end of the crusade against the Albigensians in 1244 would Philip Augustus conquer the region, while Provence remained part of the Holy Roman Empire.

It was in this region, with its profound links to the Latin world, that the troubadour culture arose, spreading through the feudal courts and guiding the tastes of late medieval Europe. At the same time, the architecture of the mendicant orders progressed rapidly, devising wide, simple, naves without aisles defined by linear

below left
Notre-Dame cathedral, begun 1276, Rodez, France

The cathedral of Rodez was burnt, left to collapse and rebuilt; the cathedral is little known among French cathedrals. The west front was originally wholly integrated into the city walls, which is why the decoration is only found on the upper parts, with a magnificent rose window and slender pinnacles.

internal surfaces inside an undecorated nave, as, for example, in the cathedral at Albi. Annexation to the French crown coincided with a period of transformation that was expressed in military architecture especially, as Aigues-Mortes and Carcassonne illustrate. Surrounded by the wide marshes of the Camargue and as the port from which the French army embarked at the time of the two crusades of Louis IX, Aigues-Mortes was one of the main commercial hubs for continental Europe and Italian maritime republics. The port, built from scratch in 1240 in an estuary near the river Rhone, enjoyed commercial rights that attracted ship-owners and merchants. The town has a quadrilateral plan arranged in an orthogonal network of streets, within a square, enclosed by turreted walls.

Ramparts and Constance Tower, 13th century, Aigues-Mortes, France

The imposing King's Tower was built during the days of Philip the Bold (1272–1289) beyond the city walls. Also known as Constance Tower (1240–1248), it was originally set up as an external fortification in the centre of a moat, with a turret that functioned as a beacon.

THE MASTERPIECE
THE PAPAL PALACE IN AVIGNON

Among the residential buildings of the 14th century, there were some in which the defensive function gradually receded to take a secondary role. In France, the exemplary masterpiece of this typology of building is the Palace in Avignon — the city on the border between the German Empire and the estates of the French crown that became the seat of the popes. It is an exceptional building in its sheer scale and complexity, built on a rocky embankment removed from the city centre and adjoining the cathedral. The first papal residence, the Palazzo Vecchio, commissioned by Benedict XII and designed by Pierre Poisson, was expressed as an austere, fortified monastery with towers and high, crenellated walls. The palace accommodates the papal apartments, chapel, buildings for the court and the conclave, all arranged around a cloister. The Palazzo Nuovo, commissioned by Clement VI (1342–1352) and designed by

Jean de Louvres, is remarkable due to its sumptuous, richly decorated interior with an innumerable succession of rooms, chapels and apartments arranged round the court of honour. There are two splendid rooms in the southern wing; in a departure from the norm they are placed over the Hall of Audiences and the Clementine chapel where the pontiff was crowned and liturgical offices were performed. Especially noteworthy are the arrangement of the service and technical quarters, particularly the large complex of kitchens and associated storage spaces was well as the organisation of the sanitary areas. Within the walls flourished the so-called 'Avignon Picturesque School', the result of the encounter between the delicate Sienese realism of Matteo Giovannetti and the graphic elegance of the French painters — marking the beginning of the expansion of Italian art into 14th century France.

Façade of the Papal Palace, 1334–1352, Avignon, France

The Papal Palace epitomises the splendour and the cultural influence of the Papal court. The palace is a building of impressive proportions, described in the chronicles of the time as "the most beautiful and most fortified dwelling in the world". Internally, the installations and internal arrangements of the palace indicate that it aimed to accommodate the highest quality of life, which was an aspect of the new social reality of Gothic culture. Externally, the palace still looks like a castle with its battlemented walls and clusters of towers and turrets. As an ensemble, the palace, connected by a bridge to the already existing urban fabric of Avignon, was an architectural microcosm enlarged to the scale of an urban nucleus.

THE MASTERPIECE
ALBI CATHEDRAL

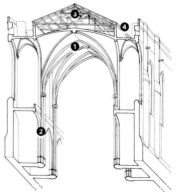

Cross-section of the Cathedral of Albi, c. 1287–1390, France

The interior of the cathedral features an aisleless single nave, rib-vaulted (1) on slender clustered piers (2). The section shows the system of timber beams in the pitched roof covering the vaulting (3) and the existence of a maintenance walkway (4).

Exterior view of the cathedral, c. 1287–1390, Albi, France

The economic and compact cathedral stands on a base with virtually no windows. The cathedral is surrounded by a continuous walkway and surmounted by a heavy tower at the west front, which gives it the appearance of a fortress. The outer walls employ a system of buttresses alternating with high, narrow, *rayonnant*–style windows, while the use of exposed brickwork creates a feeling of sculptural austerity and links the building visually to the fortified walls.

The city of Albi is the centre from which the Cathar heresy spread — the reason why the Cathars were also called the Albigensians — and it became an autonomous episcopal seignory. In a city henceforth subject to the temporal authority of the bishop and inquisitor of Languedoc, Bernard de Castanet (who flaunted his own feudal ambitions by creating a veritable citadel alongside the cathedral from 1250), on a site which dominated the neighbouring buildings — the episcopal Palace of the Berbie (1250–1300). A citadel within a city, the cathedral and episcopal palace became a huge defensive construct, uniting a cathedral consciously disguised as a fortress with the impregnability of a fortified palace (symbol of temporal power), to stand out as a garrison of religious orthodoxy in a city that had for many years been a stronghold of heresy. The architecture of the cathedral is austere and compact, contrasting with the linearism and ethereal nature of northern cathedrals. A massive donjon, or inner tower, guards the west front, fortifying the entrance to the church despite the fact that this opens into the interior of the citadel. A Late Gothic baldachin opens on the southern elevation — a magnificent portico in flamboyant style. Constructed in this way in order to resemble the castles that distinguished French territory, Sainte-Cécile looked like a royal cathedral at the time when the kings — primarily defenders of the Papacy at that time — were struggling desperately against feudal fragmentation.

THE MASTERPIECE
CARCASSONNE

Among the most important urban settlements in the history of medieval military architecture, Carcassonne, owes its present appearance to the work of 'interpretative' restoration undertaken during the course of the 19th century by Viollet-le-Duc, the restorer of medieval French buildings. The elevated city stands prominently on the crest of a hill on the right bank of the River Aude. Carcassonne reached the peak of its glory from the 12th century onwards, when the Trencavel family (Viscounts of Albi, Nîmes and Bézieres) promoted the construction of a count's palace and a cathedral within the Late Roman city walls. Refuge of the Cathars from 1209, thanks to the support of the Count of Toulouse, Carcassonne was besieged and conquered by French crusaders under the command of Simon

View of the city of Carcassonne, France

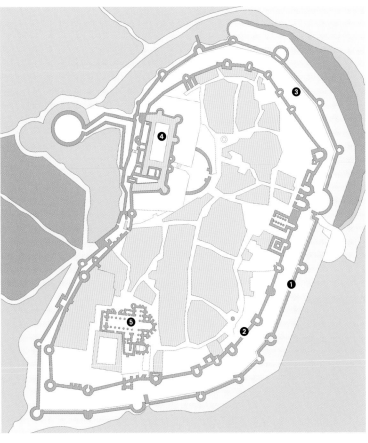

Plan of the city of Carcassonne, 13th century, France

The plan of the city is virtually an ellipse protected by two concentric rings of walls. The first circle of walls is 10 m high (1), the second 14 m (2). Both walls have walkways, battlements and embrasures. The defences feature 52 towers of different styles, i.e. square and circular.

The aperture between the two walls (*lices*) (3) was intended, in peacetime, as a place for tournaments, jousting and storing building materials. Only two gates allow access to the city — the Porte Narbonnaise (1280) and the Porte d'Aude. Enclosed within the second ring of walls are the castle (4) and the cathedral of St Nazaire (5), reconstruction of them began in 1269.

de Montfort. Under the reign of Louis IX and of Philip the Bold, three distinct building campaigns would complete the urban structuring of the city, during which time it acquired its present shape and size. By virtue of Carcassonne's strategic position, it became the seat of one of the most powerful seneschals of Languedoc, necessitating the complete restructuring of the existing defensive system, which involved the seigniorial palace, the building of a second set of walls around the city and the establishment of a settlement at the foot of the citadel on the opposite bank of the river. The section of the original that has survived the centuries gives one an idea of a fortified town in the vanguard of the period, based on the most recent innovations in construction techniques and progress in siege techniques.

THE KINGDOM OF CASTILE

The introduction of Gothic forms in the Iberian Peninsula progressed hand in hand with the process of military and political reconquest by the Christian kingdoms after the victory of Las Navas de Tolosa (1212). However, its spread encountered some resistance as the Romanesque tradition blended with technical and decorative experiments of the Islamic tradition.

However, along the pilgrimage routes, towards the latter part of the 12th century, there was already evidence of contact with northern France — whose influence can be seen in the iconography of the sculptural reliefs and in the adoption of choirs with ambulatories. The Kingdom of Castile, committed to the repopulation of lands regained from the Moors, was the kingdom culturally closest to France. It was also the most active and influential centre of that region throughout the 13th century. The construction of the cathedrals of Burgos, Toledo and León was an enterprise of major importance marked by the sheer dominance of the examples of the Île-de-France. Moreover, in Castile, a kingdom whose economy was based on agriculture, the king and the bishop were the champions of artistic progress, while the middle classes played a merely marginal role. When, around 1225, the Bishop of León promoted the building of a new cathedral, the acceptance of French methodologies in Iberia was complete. Castilian Gothic was not regarded as a mere copy or a simple importation of foreign ideas into local tradition.

Interior of Toledo Cathedral, 1222–1223, Spain

Toledo Cathedral is the largest Spanish building of the 13th century. It was an attempt to blend contemporary French architecture with motifs of Islamic origin. The aim was for the cathedral to become the religious centre of the Iberian Peninsula; it was the furthest removed from French forms revealing a desire to explore authentically Iberian solutions. Among these, one of the typological, functional and typically autochthonous characteristics which would become standard in Spanish cathedrals was the presence of a huge presbyterial area (planned as a royal funerary chapel) carved out of the ecclesiastical space and made possible by railings and barrier walls that subdivide, both visually and functionally, the unified space of the nave.

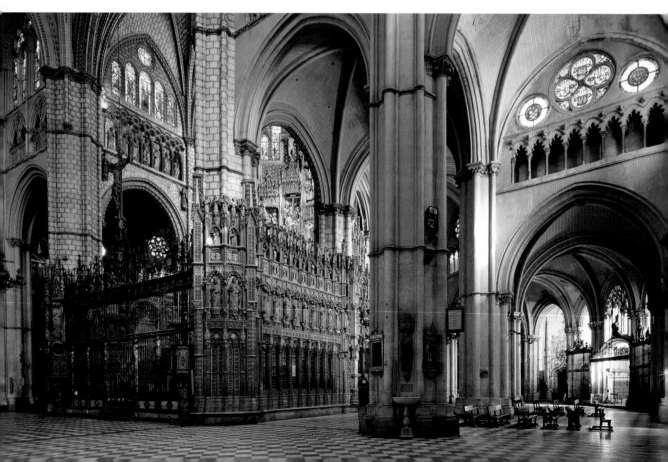

THE MASTERPIECE
BURGOS CATHEDRAL

From time to time capital of the kingdom, Burgos was an important political and religious centre situated along the road leading to France. Begun c. 1223, the cathedral was one of the main centres in Spain where French forms were truly accepted. Commissioned by Bishop Maurice, himself closely linked to the court of Ferdinand III of Castile, the cathedral boasts a floor plan with a nave and two side-aisles, a prominent transept and a choir and ambulatory. Though it looks, at first glance, like a simplification of French Gothic forms — perhaps due to economic constraints or because the huge scale of northern cathedrals remained essentially foreign in an environment still strongly tied to the Romanesque tradition — in its large forms and abundant illumination it seems, in other ways, to adhere closely to the development of Gothic architecture.

The cathedral forms the backdrop of an interesting development of monumental Gothic sculpture that, following early French models, gave rise to innovative elaborations that would influence the whole country. The wonderful Sarmental portal revived the style of French Gothic sculpture with its powerful, realistic vitality and vigorous relief work.

In the noble Late Gothic chapel of the Constable (the creation of Simon de Cologne) the ornamental parts (sculptured coats of arms, friezes, flowers, arches) became prominent elements in the whole architectural framework — an approach to architecture rooted in the overlay of Mudejar artistic traditions (Islamicized Christian art), which in the overall picture of European Gothic, ought to be recognised as a unique and distinctive trait of Spanish architecture.

View of Burgos Cathedral, late 13th–15th century, Spain

The exterior of the cathedral forms a compact whole where the different construction phases blend harmoniously. The façade is dominated by the 15th century west towers — the work of John of Cologne.

ENGLISH DECORATED GOTHIC

Between the end of the 13th and beginning of the 14th century English masons remained largely faithful to preceding models. Floor plans were extremely elongated, with projecting transepts and a central tower over the crossing, no excessive verticality in the proportions, horizontal emphasis in the façades, the retention of the 'thick wall' techniques and the reduced application of flying buttresses. Buildings of the English Decorated Gothic featured elaborate decorative forms on the surfaces of the vaulting, their design being made more complex by the addition of extra ribs (tiercerons and liernes) opening the way to Late Gothic developments.

English architects adopted geometric patterns in the window tracery in buildings for court patrons during the period between 1280–1290. These patterns were inspired directly by the latest French examples.

This rigorous observance of Rayonnant forms, whose heartland was London, saw the foundation for subsequent Perpendicular variations in the period. Further variation in the design of the tracery indicate the start of a new phase of Decorated Gothic, which came to be known as the Curvilinear Style.

The basic characteristic of this Curvilinear Style was the adoption of a linear model with curves, countercurves and ogee arches.

The impact of this feature goes beyond its mere significance in the development of the ornamental idiom, as the expression of fluidity and movement was soon extended to the three-dimensional structure of the cathedral, upsetting the concept of space and dissolving the originally solid masonry wall.

opposite page
Crossing arch of Wells Cathedral, c. 1338, Wells, England

Structural problems with the tower of Wells dictated the employment of a stone load-bearing system — most unusual for a sacred building and one which made use of techniques frequently used in building bridges. The arch entailed coupling two opposing and converging pointed arches as scissor arches.

The tower is thus read as spatially separate from the rest of the building, firstly due to the impressiveness of the structure and secondly due to the dark hue of the area in contrast with the other lighter parts; the reason for this visual separation may not be obvious. This uncommon effect, achieved by means of curves and counter curves, would be characteristic of a large part of Late Gothic work in England for a long time to come.

Octagon of Ely Cathedral, 1322–1342, England

The quest of English architecture to find different directions and new perspectives was brought to its extreme limits in the octagonal crossing of Ely Cathedral, which was the combined achievement of Alan of Walsingham, the monk and skilled goldsmith, and William Hurley, the royal carpenter. The Octagon's enormous dimensions, both in height and width, were made possible by the use of special technology. This created disconcerting, elusive and fantastic effects which placed it in the vanguard of the development of European architecture of the time. The Ely octagon is covered by a timber structure, with cantilever beams supporting a central rigid ring within the space. The lantern is raised on these beams. The ceiling is clad to look like a stone vault with tiercerons that have no load-bearing function

THE MASTERPIECE
CHAPTER HOUSES

Centrally-planned chapter houses are one of the distinctive architectural features of English medieval architecture, developing in two diametrically opposing directions: on one hand, with a richly ornamented vault due to the proliferation of tiercerons branching from a central pillar as at Lincoln Cathedral (a prototype for similar cathedrals thereafter), Canterbury Cathedral (end of 12th century), Westminster Abbey (completed in 1253), Salisbury Cathedral (post-1253) and Wells Cathedral (c. 1293–1302). On the other hand, there is the chapter house at York, considered a perfect 'glasshouse', where the wall surfaces simply 'dissolve' into enormous glazed windows. Chapter houses stand separately, generally situated near the northern arm of the transept and sometimes connected to it via a vestibule.

Chapter House vault, Lincoln Cathedral, c. late 12th century, England

The ribs curve from the slender central pillar — elegantly clustered with shafts — like the leaves of a palm tree. The structural system of the vault abandons the usual correlation between the pillar and the individual systems of the vault's framework, giving way to a more complex, unified, non-hierarchical whole created with clusters of 'nerves' which play an equal role. Figuratively speaking, the architect seems to be portraying plant forms. From a stricter design viewpoint, the architect declined to investigate the hierarchy of individual structural elements.

Chapter House vault, York Minster, c. 1290, England

The design of the octagonal Chapter House of York derives from the layout typology of English chapter houses, increasing the spatial impression by increasing the width and height of the vault and eliminating with the central support. The vault, originally to be built in stone, was in the event made of timber, reducing the weight to such an extent that the central pillar could be omitted.

The windows are carved out from the thickness of the walls, further amplifying the effect of distension and resulting in an undulating surface which, in the dazzling light streaming through the great windows, magnifies the scale of the room.

THE MASTERPIECE
YORK MINSTER

York Minster has the thin-wall framework of French Gothic with high, sharp-pointed arches. From the last quarter of the 13th century, the building underwent a campaign of restoration, making prolific use of geometric tracery in the great space of the nave. In the minster there are additions of forms unusual for England, derived from the French Rayonnant style and, in particular, some marked similarities with the cathedrals of southern France attributed to Jean de Champs.

The great transept dates back to the 13th century. Construction of the chapter house was begun in the 1260s whilst the rebuilding of the Norman nave began in the 1280s. The west towers are the most prominent feature of the west façade and were completed in 1472.

North transept of York Minster, c. 1260, England

The problem of how to deal with the ends of transepts was particularly pertinent to northern English Gothic architecture; the north transept at York being the most monumental example. Five extremely tall lancet windows (called the Five Sisters by Charles Dickens) rise over a series of blind arches. The non-figurative decoration in the transept is created by tiny coloured panes. The vault is constructed from wood. A characteristic feature of the northern English style is also a large gallery.

Exterior of York Minster from the south-east, England

Despite the clear influences of French models, and of Cologne Cathedral specifically, the proportions of York Minster are smooth, flat and primarily horizontal. The twin towers at the west end were only finished in the 15th century and they render the west end of York the most French of all English façades. In the original design they were to be incorporated in a screen-façade, as at Wells. The overall impression of horizontality is created by the choir and the nave being equal in length. The collapse of the central tower over the crossing in 1407 was a prelude to the final phase of work on the Minster, but the new lantern tower was kept at a lower height than the former one, perhaps due to the instability of the ground beneath.

ITALY

From the beginning of the 13th century, Italy had an extremely active architectural culture, one remarkably heterogeneous. Aspects of French and Burgundian styles brought in by Cistercian orders which — from the late 12th to the early 13th centuries — contributed to introducing northern forms into Italy, coexisting here with a strong Romanesque tradition and a classical inheritance kept alive by the Roman see of St Peter and by Swabian imperial influence in the south. Consequently, during the 13th century, the presence of Gothic forms and techniques in Italy was seldom to be found. The absence of a strong central power hindered the spread of a unified style and ensured that local building traditions persisted, these often being seen as representative of civic individualism. Furthermore, in almost all Italian cities, the cathedrals and, more importantly the churches, had already been renovated in the previous century and the main urban builders' yards were now completing works already begun. In the cathedrals of Modena, Parma, Cremona and Ferrara,

Façade of Ferrara Cathedral, 12th–13th century, Ferrara, Italy

The elegant façade of Ferrera Cathedral was inspired by the façade of the cathedral in Modena. The Ferrara façade is divided into three parts (tripartite) by two large buttresses similar to the one at Modena. The lower zone, including the majestic portal, is the early Romanesque nucleus. The gallery above is enclosed by arcading of blind pointed arches which communicate a different idiom and form a loggia walkway separating the external marble cladding from the masonry at the rear. The second loggia and the three Gothic gables were built in the 13th century.

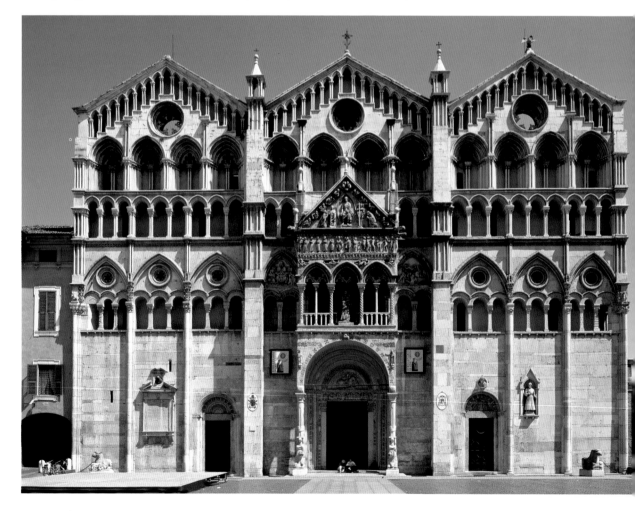

Cathedral façade, begun 1308, Orvieto, Italy

The stonemasons' yard at Orvieto Cathedral, headed by Lorenzo Maitani, represented an architectural event as important for the cultural education of the clients as it was for their craftsmen. The complex design process of the façade — independent and unrelated to the rest of the building — was symptomatic of the emergence of a new cultural ethos. Conceived as an architectural component completely divorced from the body of the church behind it, it has a layout based on a geometric system of squares and triangles and their interrelations and intersections. The façade is a masterpiece of 'ornamental Gothic' — renovated in a French manner — observed in the tracery, rose window, spires and pinnacles which are reminiscent of the intricate art of the goldsmith. The façade stands in a direct relationship with the surrounding city space, influencing one's perception of it.

where work was in its final stages, there were indeed some modern features incorporated — but not such as to alter the impression of the original space — while the volumes retain their compact and balanced character. In Italy, the embrace of pure surface values, the dematerialisation and thinness of the walls, led to alternative thinking about planning, parallel to the elaboration of French Gothic, with special focus to the effects of an expanding perspective. It was primarily the mendicant orders who would inspire this kind of architecture. After the 1240s, Italian builders began to construct religious buildings of great scale but that were, nevertheless, simple in structure. During the 14th century in Italy, there was a surge of building activity, both public and private — the result and expression of the renewal of urban areas and the buildings connected with them. All kinds of different organisations promoted this development: governing bodies, major charitable foundations, the Church and the mendicant orders, political and corporate organisations as well as the great patrician families. It should also be remembered that the transfer of the popes to Avignon favoured the strengthening of local territorial powers. In Italian cities, more than elsewhere, the issue of urban landownership was seen as a political rather than a social problem. This

Saint Mary of the Thorn, begun 1325, Pisa, Italy

The small oratory, Saint Mary of the Thorn, was built in the 13th century on the banks of the River Arno. The oratory was modified and extended in the following century according to a design by Lupo di Francesco to house a fragment of Christ's crown of thorns. Always under threat by river flooding, the small church underwent numerous restorations until it was finally dismantled in 1871, piece by piece, and rebuilt on higher terrain. Completely enveloped in marble casing with duo-colour stripes, the church is adorned with rose windows, finials, spires and tabernacles, as well as many ornamental sculptures.

opposite page
Nave of Florence Cathedral (St Maria del Fiore), begun 1366, Italy

Resumption of work on the *duomo* of Florence, interrupted in 1337 after the death of the chief architect, reveals a great deal about the relationship between the clients and the workers in a masons' yard under a strong urban influence. The early scheme, by Arnolfo di Cambio, was founded on the rational relationship between the central plan of the east end and the more straightforward longitudinal body. Onto this, Francesco Talenti superimposed a new design, similar in conception though larger and loftier. The construction of the cathedral was the result of a complex and integrated system of skills and responsibility in which the political authorities, both administrative and fiscal, (the powerful Wool Guild), intervened as protagonists in the dual roles of funding and controlling

fact helps us to gain a better understanding of the reasoning behind certain technical and stylistic choices made by architects and clients in the course of the century.

The rejection of external buttressing in the form of flying buttresses was a primary and outstanding characteristic of Italian Gothic, (excluding Milan Cathedral and the church of St Francis at Bologna). What prevailed, both in religious and secular architecture, was the ribbed vaulting of the roof, over square bays, naves and aisles of more or less the same height. To ensure the structural stability of the building, the external wall was thickened in some places in a manner that the volumetric impact of the forms, compact and well defined, was in harmony with the other elements of the urban landscape. The different Gothic architectural language chosen in Italy as compared with France is clear. It is reasonable to believe that resistance to importing foreign solutions and prototypes might have been due to their proud awareness of their own civic independence and to the specific urban values and context of a given city.

THE MASTERPIECE
UPPER CHURCH OF THE BASILICA OF ST FRANCIS, ASSISI, ITALY

The history of the construction and the structure of the complex were integral with its triple function: as a sepulchral church, a conventual church and as a Papal chapel. The double-storey plan was dictated by the steep slope of the topography and was designed in order to guarantee that the façade facing the town enjoyed the desired pre-eminence.

Whereas the lower basilica (1) adhered to a late Romanesque style, the upper church (2) was a new entity in which the abundance of Gothic features (tracery, linearity of supports, adoption of the skeleton structure) indicate a direct derivation from France, not only in the workforce active on site, but also due to a specific request from the clients, who wanted to uphold a symbolic monument of Franciscanism, i.e. give the order a modern and international image boost.

Nevertheless, Rome remained an important point of reference, as can be seen in the rich pictorial adornment and in the orientation of the façade towards Jerusalem; as at St Peter's Basilica. In the mid-13th century, Pope Innocent IV, having returned from a long sojourn in France, issued a calling for the decoration of the basilica, which was considered somewhat bare and in need of adornment.

The first alterations are to be found in the 'typological' windows in the apse, linking the Old and New Testaments through parallel illustrations on moments in the life of Christ and His apostles.

Between 1297 and 1299, Giotto painted his famous frescoes on the walls of the basilica depicting events from the life of St Francis, thereby marking a decisive turning point in the history of painting.

Cross-section of the Basilica of St Francis, 1228–1253, Assisi, Italy

This section illustrates the upper basilica (2) and the lower (1), from where there is access into the crypt below, where the tomb of St Francis contains (3).

opposite page
Interior of the upper Basilica of St Francis, 1228–1253, Assisi, Italy

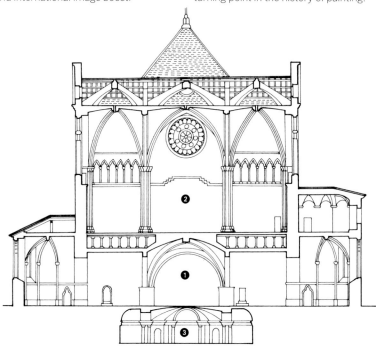

PALAZZI PUBBLICI, LOGGIAS AND MARKETS

Whereas cathedrals sought to establish a visual presence in cities by means of monumentality, the crenelated outlines of *palazzi pubblici* loomed over urban landscapes as symbols of civic power. The built form was to fulfil a desire for prestige that marked the ever more lavish and expensive projects of all echelons of society, both ecclesiastical and lay. Between the 13th and 14th centuries, a new type of architecture arose that would become typical of the urban landscape and the object of special attention; namely the *palazzo pubblico*, the seat of civic government. Its acquisition of functional and symbolic importance produced a fundamental urban transformation. Gradually the narrow focus on civic and religious activity concentrated solely on the cathedral in the 11th and 12th centuries gave way to the division of the roles of civic and religious power as each became stabilised and differentiated.

Urban power was then divided between the cathedral and the *palazzo pubblico*, both overlooking the large, open *piazza*. To these buildings we might add a third communal space, which was exclusively used as a market.

The typical form of *palazzo pubblico* in the Po Valley was the *broletto*. This was

Palazzo Pubblico, begun 1281, Piacenza, Italy

The *Gotico*, as the old *palazzo pubblico* in Piacenza is called, is a splendid example of civic Lombard architecture of the 13th century. The palazzo was commissioned by Alberto Scoto, representative of the Guelph bourgeoisie and ruler of the city.

After the northern side was built, the works were interrupted due to the economic depression which followed the plague. The palazzo follows the Lombard *broletto* style and has a deep gallery with two aisles of white, red and grey marble. The upper gallery part, made from terracotta, is adorned with graceful three-pane windows, a remarkable rose window and cornices with arches and merlons. Its purpose was to accommodate popular assemblies.

generally organised on two levels: the lower being open and with porticoes, the upper closed and comprising a capacious assembly chamber with large windows and balconies overlooking the square. Inside, the walls of the great council chambers were completely covered with allegorical murals, such as are still to be admired in town-halls in Sienna and Padua. In central Italy, the eternal struggle between Guelph cities (allies of the Pope, e.g. Florence) and Ghibelline cities (allies of the emperor, e.g. Sienna) was translated into *palazzi pubblici* being well fortified and almost inaccessible as portrayed in their massive exterior, clearly built in turbulent times.

Italian cities became the centre of a highly dynamic social life, where mercantile activity dominated urban economic life. Owning a dwelling did not automatically confer right of citizenship, which could only be obbined by being a member and playing a part in mercantile organisations, which represented the highest social class where all the mobile capital was held. The favoured form of organising work was corporative. Arts and craft guilds were established, developing out of associations initially created by artisans for religious and charitable purposes. In their more complex forms, mercantile orders were transformed into professional cartels with profit acquisition as their primary goal. The evermore powerful guilds gained recognition of their autonomy with systems of self-government and their own statutes to regulate the exercise of trades. The citizen there by gained material prosperity, obtained political rights and shared in the government of the commune. Thus, among the most important civic structural aspects that sealed the image of cities were the loggias, administrative bases and meeting places of the guilds.

Palazza della Ragione, 13th-14th century, Padua, Italy

During the Gothic period, the city of Padua enjoyed a period of particular glory that is reflected in its urban structure. Between the end of the 13th century and the beginning of the 14th century numerous lay and ecclesiastical buildings (e.g. basilica of St Anthony, 1232–1310) were constructed. The Palazzo della Ragione, which housed the judicial court, was built in 1218–1219. The main block, constructed in terracotta, is elongated and extends over two storeys, the lower storey being arcaded. The Gothic renovation (1306–1309) carried out by Fra Giovanni of the Eremitani, comprised raising and thickening the walls, an ogee roof clad in lead, as well as an impressive colonnade with an open gallery above that runs down the long side walls.

left
Loggia del Bigallo, 1352–1358, Florence, Italy

Built by the Company of St Mary of Mercy, this loggia originally served to give refuge to lost or abandoned children. On the ground floor, the loggia houses an oratory, while the upper floor, which has two-pane windows, was intended as a refuge for foundlings.

Antonio di Vincenzo and Lorenzo da Bagnomarino, exterior and detail of the Loggia della Mercanzia, 1384–1391, Bologna, Italy

Built for the commercial life of the town, the Loggia della Mercanza houses the mercantile excise office, the seats of several corporations and the merchants' forum. Above the elegant open arcade with pointed arches, there is a small, canopied balcony closely flanked by a pair of graceful two-paned windows and surmounted by Ghibelline swallow-tailed merlons. The presence of several guilds is clear from the inclusion of their emblems in the upper part of the façade. Among them is the Tailors' Guild which has a pair of scissors as the symbol of their trade. The loggia was rebuilt after the Second World War.

Palazzo dei Priori, c. 1296, Perugia, Italy

The result of successive stages of building, the Palazzo dei Priori documents the politico-administrative evolution of the city, culminating in 1303 with the institution of the city magistracy of the Priors. Built around the old core of the residence of the Captain of the People, the palazzo is a clear, decorative building embellished with a sequence of three-paned windows punctuating the façade. The elevation facing the square has an elegant doorway surmounted by a griffin and a lion on a bracket — the symbols of Perugia and the Guelph party respectively.

VENICE

The acceptance and the independent development of the Gothic architectural idiom in Venice went hand in hand with a number of major changes: the city's rise as a great maritime power, its role as a unique link between West and East, the structure of its society and institutions and its urban growth — at the turn of the 14th century, Venice had approximately 115,000 inhabitants.

Though the introduction of Gothic elements was already noticeable during the course of the 13th century, it was only by the mid-14th century that their mature adoption was witnessed. This occurred when the building sites of conventual blocks opened out and brought public and private projects into being that overtook the entire area of St Mark's Basin. Thanks to the dominant aristocratic oligarchy, who were endeavouring to strengthen the city's economic role as well as its image, a type of urban *palazzo* developed that would remain almost unchanged down the centuries: a grand dwelling often adopting a U-shaped floor plan with a courtyard enclosed on three sides, tangential to the *portego*. This ensures that the rooms were well lit and that the courtyard became the hub of domestic life. In Venetian Late Gothic palaces, the importance of the grand reception room on the *piano nobile* was constantly emphasised. The façade of the building had an elegant series of multi-pane windows, which occupied the central part of the façade and acted as a formal compositional fulcrum. The decorative style of Byzantine origin, the erudite quotation of Islamic motifs and the use of expensive materials were all responsible for the graphic embellishment of the front façade of residential buildings overlooking the water. From the 1330s onwards, the mendicant orders also began to build their convents in the lagoon city, about a century later than in other Italian cities.

bottom, left
Ca' d'Oro, 1421–1440, Venice, Italy

The Ca' d'Oro commissioned by Mario Contarini — a member of one the most prestigious Venetian families — embodies many of the characteristics of Venetian Late Gothic civil architecture. The starting point for the design was the canal frontage, the design of which becomes a dialogue between the *chiaroscuro* interplay of the multi-light windows and the dominance of the solid wall surfaces. The sculptor, Matteo Raverti, revived the idea of an open loggia on the *piano nobile*, drawing on the repertoire of flamboyant Gothic. The surfaces are clad in rare marbles, which offset the materiality of the brick building, transfiguring the façade into symbolic values of light.

bottom right
Nave of the Church of St Maria Gloriosa dei Frari, 1334, Venice, Italy

The Frari Church uses a system of interior reinforcement based on timber bracing (trusses) that connect the pillars to one another, lengthways and crossways, linking the latter to the side walls. This system produces the interesting effect of creating a three-dimensional modulation of space notable for spreading uniform, diffuse light throughout.

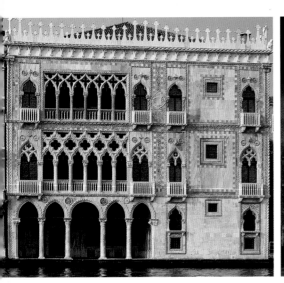

THE MASTERPIECE
THE DOGE'S PALACE

The completion of the façade of the Doge's Palace in 1424 brought to an end a building site established around eighty years previously. The construction of the Grand Council assembly chamber became a factor of architectural significance.

The overall impression of the façade is the result of the contrast between the two lower levels — open to the outside with porticos superimposed over one another — and the upper level with its completely covered surfaces. Individual architectural elements (pillars, capitals, arcades, ogival arches) return to Gothic floral forms of an exuberant Venetian kind. The façade is symbolic of Venetian figurative theory, a style made of light and chromatic effects, which dematerialise the surfaces. The strict fidelity of the 15th century Doge's Palace to the style of the preceding century — at a time when Florence had already opened the way to the Renaissance — justified the validity and nobility of Venetian Late Gothic intended to honour the tradition, a factor which contributed to the stability and the grandeur of Venice.

External façade of the Doge's Palace, 1422–1424, Venice, Italy

SIENNA

The Campo and Palazzo Pubblico, late 12th century, Sienna, Italy

Among the most architecturally note-worthy medieval urban environments is the Campo in Sienna, which was built between the 13th and 14th centuries at a time when the city, then a free commune, reached its height of splendour and wanted to showcase a public space. The particular configuration of the square — divided into nine segments by radiating lines symbolizing the Government of the Nine — was adapted to suit the terrain thus taking the convex shape of a shell. The Campo is determined by the positions of the Palazzo Pubblico and the adjacent buildings that surround it.

The visual centre of the space, the Palazzo, was built from the late 13th century and was then surrounded by the private residences of the nobility. The Mangia (Eater's) Tower (1325–1348) was built as a communal symbol which, by its vertical thrust, counterbalances the volume of the Palazzo. The Piazza Chapel is situated on the ground level; it was built in 1348 following a vow made to try and ward off the plague.

During the course of the 12th century Sienna was at the centre of international communications, with a growing economy and population prompting it to adopt communal laws of a consular code and to inaugurate a policy of territorial expansion. In the following century, the great political, urban and artistic period flourished which imbued the city the architectural characteristics that still distinguish it to this day.

The systematisation of a bipolar structure around which city life and urban structures revolved dates from this time — the political sphere being the area of the Piazza del Campo and the religious sphere the great structure of the cathedral. The Sienese Campo is the seat and symbol of civic power. It stands in the ancient market area on a curved shell-like slope terminated by the City Hall (*palazzo comunale*), which underwent an architectural transformation from a fortress of the feudal type into an elegant palazzo — the seat of public administration and governing bodies.

The religious centre is situated on the most ancient settlement of Sienna, Castelvecchio, and revolves around the cathedral — which underwent radical reconstruction during the 13th century. The pre-existing cathedral became part of the city's most ambitious architectural project: the construction of a new cathedral, where the old one formed the transept of the new one. Begun in 1339, work stopped shortly after construction commenced either due to the plague or due to economic and structural problems. This has left its indelible mark on the enormous, incomplete façade, as well as in the remains of the huge nave — both symbols of glory and decay alike.

THE MASTERPIECE
SIENNA CATHEDRAL

Though consecrated in 1179, work continued on the cathedral all through the 13th century, when the position of the façade was chosen and the cupola (1263) and bell tower (1264) were completed.

The façade is clad externally with a black and white marble cladding, which references the city's coat of arms. There is some doubt as to exactly who directed the work. The presence of Nicola Pisano, who constructed the cathedral pulpit, is presumed in the early phase. He was succeeded by his son Giovanni (1284–1296), who is credited with the lower section of the façade, famous for its three, deeply splayed portals. The upper section was constructed from 1377 on by Giovanni di Cecco, who adopted a triple gable arrangement probably borrowed from Orvieto Cathedral, which is characterised by the decorative forms of floriated Gothic. The building manifests the use of geometric proportions based on the pure forms of the equilateral triangle, the square and the circle — a modular grid system that provides a rational system to the structure.

Exterior and nave of the Duomo, 12th–15th century, Sienna, Italy

Above the spacious interior of the cathedral a two-level elevation is articulated, one above the other, and separated by a robust 15th century cornice which features portraits of the Popes in a continuous sequence of round arches below and wide windows of the clerestory above. The interior is clad in alternating bands of white and black marble, which enhance and increase the effects of light and enliven the nave.

THE CASTLES OF FREDERICK II

During the 13th century, building activity in the south of Italy — driven by the policies of Hohenstaufen Emperor, Frederick II of Swabia (1220–1250) — focused mainly on residential and military architecture and was intended to affirm the visible presence of the sovereign in the territory as well as to establish an organic network of defensive settlements and control, conveying a message of strength and imperial sovereignty. In southern Italy and Sicily, traditional building styles usually reflected Eastern models: Byzantine and Arab. From a architectural genre viewpoint, these buildings belong to the Romanesque tradition of building.

However, by the close of the 1220s Gothic forms had started to be incorporated, especially in decorative and structural details such as capitals, windows and vaults. This development was thanks to the input of Cistercian builders, from whom the use of the square as a construction module came; probably through the lessons learned from the architecture of the knightly orders. The typological genre on which Frederick's castles were based was indeed the crusader castle. Between the 12th and 13th centuries the crusader castle formed a sort of experimental laboratory for the West's methodology of fortification, a necessity in the face of Islamic military technology. Another component of Frederick II's style was the classical use of Roman masonry techniques (ashlar curtain walls, *opus reticulatum*) and the collection and the reuse of old materials. Utilising this classical style had a clear political and instrumental significance as an assertion of imperial ideology.

Castello Maniace, 1232–1240, Syracuse, Sicily

The castle, situated on the far tip of the island, was commissioned by Frederick II and built with clean and functional lines that reflected the emperor's taste — a perfect square in floor plan layout with four round towers one situated at each corner. Constructed from volcanic lava, limestone and sandstone, the fortress was initially only accessible via a drawbridge and was surrounded by a moat, which made it impregnable. Despite being damaged in the 1693 earthquake, the castle's 13th century external structure remains intact.

Castel del Monte, c. 1240, Andria, Italy

The extraordinary configuration of Castel del Monte is a synthesis of different aspects of Frederician artistic culture; its complexity contrasting with the clean geometry of its structure. Castel del Monte translates Cistercian Gothic into castle form, noble and classical, based on a geometric shape — an octagon — which not only has strong symbolic impact but is also reminiscent of the cathedral pulpit and the fountains in the town square. There was clearly a desire to pursue an ideal of abstract beauty with the aim of conveying a sense of imperial grandeur. The octagon gives form to the imperial idea, referring to significant details, ranging from the shape of the Swabian crown and baptisteries and shrines — interwoven with the ideas of rebirth and eternity — to the Dome of the Rock in Jerusalem, San Vitale at Ravenna and the Palatine chapel in Aachen.

The octagon is thus linked to the concept of royalty originating in God. It also represents cosmic equilibrium, the nautical wind-rose and the union between heaven and earth. In the interior of the building, several precise numerical relationships are referenced. Variously interpreted as a military building, a hunting lodge or an astronomical observatory (the precision of its calculations can be verified at the solstices), the castle is built as a regular octagon around an internal courtyard with two superimposed floors. Each consists of eight identical rooms with octagonal turrets above. Placed between heaven and earth, the castle symbolises the perfection of the emperor through the harmony of form, numeric and naturalistic detail.

THE FINAL YEARS
OF THE MIDDLE AGES

The 15th century saw the consolidation of the Flamboyant Style, a variant of French Gothic, which is characterised by the embellishment of technical and decorative features, though without any major structural innovations. The style is already identifiable in the decorative schemes visible on the upper part of the façade of Rouen cathedral (begun 1370) where wavy curves and counter-curves create an effect of flames. Flamboyant architecture abandoned the emphasis on structural lines in the various frameworks — the principle which had regulated the main phases of the Gothic period of architecture — in favour of organic plant forms alongside similar naturalistic features typical of French artistic output at the time. The Flamboyant Style found its finest expression, above all, in façades featuring abundant wimpergs, curving and counter-curving patterns, freestanding aedicules, creating a dynamic interplay of planes that vary according to where the observer is standing.

The result is a visually constantly shifting scene in a manner which utilised every opportunity possible to present richly decorative and fantastic subject matter. Within the buildings, there was a tendency to invent unusual and quirky solutions for points where ribs, vaults and pillars intersected. Meanwhile, interest in innovative geometric and typological structural arrangements waned. The quest for the freedom to find maverick solutions, and the surprise effects produced by them, was an approach to design that applied to different buildings and regions. This approach was most often adopted in architecture commissioned by the courts or by members of the ecclesiastical hierarchy.

Hôtel de Cluny, 1485–1498, Paris

In some parts of Europe, the final phase of the medieval experience spread, not only throughout the 15th century, but also into the first decades of the 16th century. In Italy, the birth of Renaissance culture was already evident and widely diffused. In Britain, where there was an acute economic and financial crisis, the architectural policy of the House of York was to flaunt their wealth — creating a magnificent and polished image of their realm. Thus, in the 15th century, English architecture emphasised its interests in decorative styles, providing a clear and functional response to the renewed interest in various types of formalism. In Germany, the most interesting architectural idea was the complex vaulting in stucco, which made use of sharp arrises in

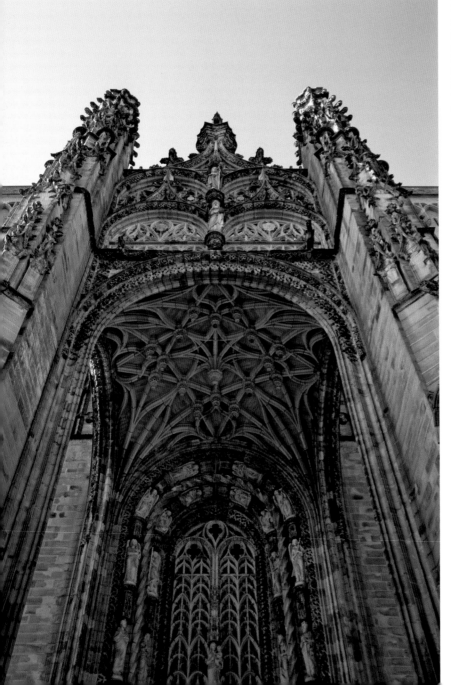

Baldachin of Albi Cathedral, 1520–1535, France

Lacework in stone — the portico of the right-hand side entrance of Albi cathedral is also called a 'baldachin'. Sumptuously adorned with pinnacles, spires and foliage, the entrance boasts a most wonderful Flamboyant vault with ribs tracing curves and counter-curves.

opposite page, left
Great stair tower of Albrechtsburg , begun 1471, Meissen, Germany

The rotation of the spiral staircase affects all the architectural parts — the significance of the columns is reduced, their angular segments lost in the mass of the vaulting. The effect of an architecture that attempts to imitate wooden carving is increased by the configuration of the vaults, where the parts left in plaster terminate either in profiled ribs or folded sharp-edged ribs. Unforeseen and surprising spatial effects emerge as they are centred on the dynamism derived from a novel use of geometric solids.

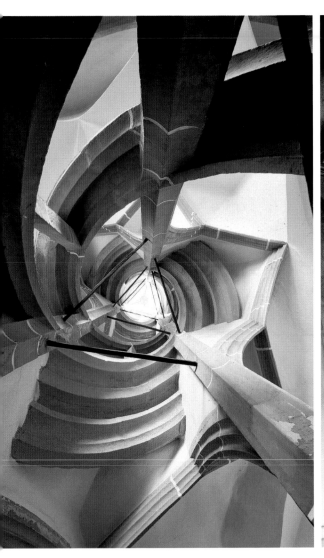

an angular style. This method of vaulting transformed the surface by means of deep concave features that gave the impression of folded paper or carved wood. In Italy, over and above the profound diversity of its social, political, territorial and cultural network, the search for identity tended towards a unifying frame of reference, revisiting the themes and forms of the ancient world. This quest led to the Renaissance and a clear ideological classification that would give the Gothic ideal a negative reputation. The Bohemian region witnessed a new chapter in Late Gothic architecture in the area of the German Empire when the structural, spatial and decorative potential implicit in the poetic style of the architect/sculptor, Peter Parler, was revisited and further developed by Benedikt Ried, one of the greatest architects working between the end of the 15th and the start of the 16th century. When Vladislav Jagellon, King of Bohemia, launched the reconstruction of Prague Castle in 1483, he hoped to reaffirm the prestige of the place and to guarantee the sovereign a degree of comfort, so he placed the court architect, Ried, in charge. Ried rose to the challenge and created his most significant work here — the impressive Vladislav Hall.

Benedikt Ried, Vladislav's Hall, 1493–1515, Hradčany, Prague, Czech Republic

The largest room in Central Europe of the period is enclosed by a vault extending from wall to wall with no intermediate supports and with flowing, intertwining ribs. The curvaceous lines conceal the precise geometric construction of the surfaces and make it impossible to discern the role, structural or decorative, they play in the whole architectural scheme.

**following pages
Sculptures adorning the exterior of Gloucester Cathedral, mid-14th century, England**

PRAGUE: THE FOUNDING OF AN IMPERIAL CITY

Charles IV of Luxemburg became Holy Roman Emperor in 1349. He chose to live in Prague, which, at his request, had already been made an episcopal see in 1344 by Pope Clement VI. Following Charles IV's ascent to the throne at his initiative, the city assumed the role of imperial capital, transforming it into a highly important centre of cultural and artistic development thus acquiring the fascinating and unique appearance that still distinguishes Prague today. The city was the seat of the first university in central Europe, endowed with an important college, the Carolinum (from 1348). Major construction work commenced, most notably on the new cathedral of St Vitus, in the upper part of the city within the castle walls (Hradčany). The political and building programme Charles IV chose to define his capital in a completely new way altered the role of the River Moldava. Up until that time, the river had formed the boundary (as had been established in negotiations between royal settlements and the burgher city) between the two most ancient centres of the city. Changes in existing relationships caused by the creation of a third urban centre — the little town of Malá Strana at the foot of the castle, a pivot linking the imperial residential zone with the influential burgher zone beyond the river, whose centre was the Gothic bulk of the town hall and Tyn Church facing each other across the Old Town Square — transformed Prague into a tripartite city. Therefore the need arose for a large, solid, connecting masonry bridge; thus the construction of the famous Charles Bridge.

bottom left
Karlstejn Castle, 1348–1357,
Prague, Czech Republic

The impressive Karlstejn Castle is attributed to the architects, Matthew of Arras and Peter Parler and is situated a few miles from Prague. The castle was the preferred residence of Charles IV — a refuge the Emperor could withdraw to and a stronghold to store the crown jewels securely. It was erected on the summit of a crag as a clear symbol of the emperor's power, with three massive rectangular towers perched on the hill.
The original complex was partially rebuilt in the 19th century.

opposite page, right
Town Hall astronomical clock, 1410, Prague, Czech Republic

The presence of a mechanical clock was a symbol of the city's wealth and prestige, not only for the financial investment involved, but also for the high cost of maintenance.
An astronomical clock adorns the façade of the ancient Town Hall in the old city (Staré Mesto) in Prague. The *Orloj* consists of two quadrants. The lower quadrant displays the signs of the zodiac and the months of the year. In the upper quadrant, the hands move across symbols of the sun, moon and stars, against a background of blue (daytime), brown (dusk) and black (nighttime). At the close of each hour, a procession of the twelve apostles proclaims the time and the allegorical figures alongside the quadrants (Vanity, Avarice, Turkish Invader and Death) come to life. A crowing cock announces the end of the spectacle.

Peter Parler, Charles Bridge, 1357, Prague, Czech Republic

A grandiose piece of public infrastructure, this famous majestic bridge traces a slightly curving course across the Vltava River and is based on sixteen supports spanned by arches. A tower at each end controls entry to the bridge. In keeping with the urban customs of the time, the bridge would become one of the symbolic structures of the city, combining social, commercial and judicial functions. It was also an urban axis along which, on ceremonial occasions, imperial processions wound their way.

THE MASTERPIECE
ST VITUS'S CATHEDRAL

The building of the new cathedral of St Vitus in Prague was begun in 1344. The cathedral was designed and supervised by French architect, Matthew of Arras, who specified an apse and choir with ambulatory and radial chapels, adopting a traditional arrangement and construction. The cathedral's great improvement — which made it the first clear example in Europe of a new way of thinking about Gothic architecture — occurred in 1352 when, following the death of Matthew, control of the construction site passed to 23-year-old Peter Parler, who confidently modified what had already been built at the east end of the building. In addition to grafting on the sacristy building and Wenceslas Chapel, the key alterations in the ground floor plan amounted to an innovative system of vaulting adopted throughout most of the church, with stellar and triangular rib patterns and the insertion of flying arches (ribs 'suspended in the air') or pendant semi-arches held in place by tie rods. Altogether, it created a programme of formal choices that critics generally consider as being English in origin.

Equally innovative was the treatment of the walls, which completely changed the logic of the original plan by placing a strong emphasis on the geometric features framing the lesser components. The concatenation of individual parts became more complex through the use of oblique surfaces. This produced the visual effect of a wavering space, hollow towards the windows, so that the openings were given lead elements in the quest for continuity that typified the whole.

opposite page
Detail of the triforium and clerestory of St Vitus's Cathedral, 1374–1385, Prague, Czech Republic

Between 1374 and 1385, Peter Parler turned his hand to constructing the triforium and clerestory of the cathedral of St Vitus. The triforium has a pierced parapet situated in front of the shafts and obliquely placed masonry partitions linking the surface of the windows with the foreground plane, into which windows are inserted as in the clerestory above.

Apsidal view of St Vitus's Cathedral, 1344–1352, Prague, Czech Republic

The choir of St Vitus was initially the work of Matthew of Arras, who designed the floor plan and started work on a part of the ambulatory and ring of chapels. Peter Parler's subsequent interventions (the buttresses and clerestory) created a revolutionary spirit on the contemporary architectural scene. The dominant verticality of the composition is enhanced by the elongation of the pinnacles on the buttresses which perforate the eaves.

AN ARCHITECTURAL DYNASTY: THE PARLER FAMILY

During the Middle Ages, the term *parler* ('to speak' in French) or *parlier* designated that professional figure who, while the master builder was absent from the construction site, was charged with the job of translating the architect's design into stone. In the 14th century, Parler became a surname. From that time on, the Parlers would form one of the most important architectural families of the 14th century. It is to them that we owe much of the architectural development in central Eastern Europe.

The founder of the family, who is documented in various sources, was Heinrich I the Old. He was trained in the masons' yard of Cologne Cathedral and emigrated later to Schwäbisch Gmünd to build the nave of Holy Cross Church. There he inaugurated a new type of architecture that would profoundly influence subsequent Austro-German architectural development. Among his sons, Peter (born 1330) figured at the forefront on the stage of Late European Gothic. Trained in his father's yard, he worked in Strasbourg, Cologne and Nuremberg before taking charge of the yard at Prague Cathedral. Peter, himself, had two sons: Wenzel was appointed architect of Vienna Cathedral in 1400–1404 and John IV was, with Jacob, responsible for building the choir of Kutná Hora in Bohemia.

opposite page, left
Choir of the church of the Holy Cross, begun 1351, Schwäbisch Gmünd, Germany

Holy Cross Church marks the early start of German Late Gothic and its definitive dominance over the French Rayonnant forms. The nave and the choir have different systems of ribs — a combination of vaults with a stellar pattern and lozenges in the nave and a crowded and undifferentiated lozenge system with small ribs in the choir — which shows that they belong to two different cultural worlds and can be attributed to different architects. The choir is the work of Heinrich Parler the elder, whilst the nave is attributed to his son, Peter.

Bust of Peter Parler, St Vitus's Cathedral, c. 1370, Prague, Czech Republic

The portrait busts of the two architects, Matthew of Arras (1344–1352) and Peter Parler (1356–1399) on Prague Cathedral raised the rank of the master builders to be on a par with those of the emperor and his family, the first archbishops of Prague and the administrators of the builders' yard. The originality and creativity of the design process of Peter Parler stood out from early on through the great freedom of his solutions in mapping out the ribs of the vaults, all based on exact geometric laws. It is not coincidental that the distinctive symbol of the family is the stylized outline of a square, as can be seen on his robe. Parler made a clear break with French Rayonnant Gothic, looking instead to England and northern Germany for inspiration.

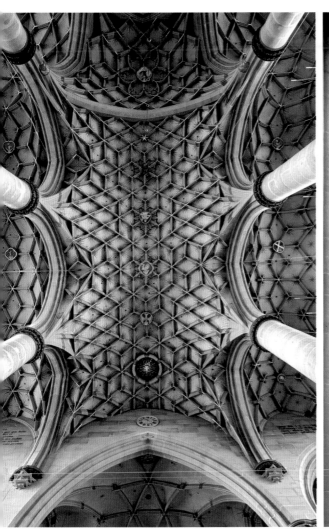

The presence of another member of the family in the yard at Milan Cathedral, Henry III, is documented in 1392. Although there were Parlers present in all the major builders' yards of the time, we should not make the mistake of thinking there was a consistent style in the work of this family of architects, even though there are some consistencies that would justify use of the adjective 'parlerian'. Peter's direct or indirect influence was more general than that of his family and would extend to many centres in the Bohemian, Austro-German and Tyrolean regions, even as far as Brabant and Flanders.

The extraordinary innovations of the Parler family were still in use in the Late Gothic architecture of German-speaking countries in the mid-15th century. The new and original configurations of the vaults affected the perception of space because the construction was planned precisely to make such effects possible. It is because of 'parlerian' experimentation that, around the end of the 15th century, the architecture of German countries achieved contemporary forms, only to then be halted by the influences of the Reformation and the slow penetration of Italian Renaissance models. Religious building activity slowed down as a result of the Reformation, while Italian models led to stylistic confusion and contradiction.

St Barbara's Church, begun 1388, Kutná Hora, Czech Republic

Commissioned to Jakob Parler by the local Miners' Guild in 1388, St Barbara's was finished in 1512 by architect, Benedikt Ried, an innovator in the Parler tradition. He placed a second higher level above the original floor plan of a nave and double aisles at the first level with single aisles, covering the whole structure with a single vaulting system consisting of intertwined ribs, adorned with flowers. The church, is a marvellous example of German Late Gothic and creates a multi-dimensional and multi-directional space.

Vaulting and plan of St Anna's Church, 1499–1525, Annaberg, Poland

The floor plan of St Anna's reveals how the buttresses are carried into the interior of the church (1), where they fluidly penetrate the celebrated vaulting. The complex layout of the ribs is invaluable proof of the artistic freedom of German Late Gothic architects, whose point of reference was the Vladislav Hall by Benedikt Ried. The vaulting scheme — prominent but slender, similar to timber laminas — is the result of a highly original and graphic study based on intersection of sinuous, organic lines: the flower-petal design of the ribs meandering in every direction (2), the flow towards the pillars still echoing plant forms and the metamorphosis of the aisles into knots and arabesques (3).

opposite page
North aisle, Collegiate Church of St Blaise, 1469–1474, Brunswick, Germany

The Parler School made its presence felt throughout Germanic regions. The renovations carried out in St Blaise in the 15th century juxtapose the modernity of the double northern aisle alongside the ancient building, without deferring to the extant original Romanesque forms — a series of circular piers whose shafts are imaginatively created by four spiral shafts.

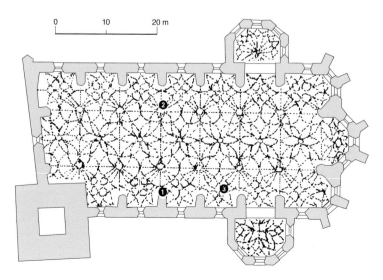

THE MASTERPIECE
THE CATHEDRAL, MILAN

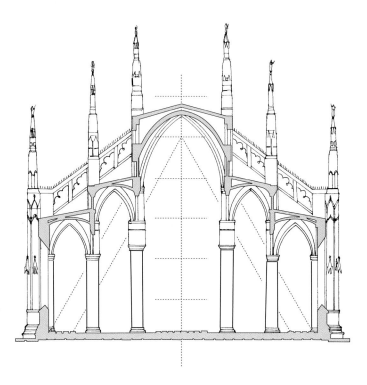

Cross-section of Milan Cathedral, begun 1387, Italy

The suggestions of Piacenza mathematician, Gabriele Stornaloco, consulted in 1391 along with a number of international *maestri*, show how the knowledge of geometry and mathematics had become a central element in the training of architects. The section clearly illustrates the problem of the dimensions of Milan cathedral which, although formally adhering to a Gothic style of French derivation, still adopts traditional massive proportions based on an equilateral triangle, thus defining the scale and proportions of the nave and aisles.

The masons' yard at Milan Cathedral, begun by the Visconti family in 1387, provided an opportunity for the comparison and fusion of techniques from various provenances. All techniques focused on finding the optimum solution to employ for the crossing, in view of the planned construction of a high spire on which to place the Virgin's statue.

In order to solve the technical building problems, a number of *maestri* (masters) were given a hearing — from the Italian, Campionesi and French, Nicolas de Bonneaventure and Jean Mignot to German, Henry Parler III. Although not unusual, the procedure adopted in Milan appears to have been exceptional precisely in its appeal to an international panel of architects, perhaps to be explained by the Viscontis' desire to gain prominence as a great ruling European house, cultivating a non-regional and slightly retrospective approach at the Cathedral.

The methodology chosen for Milan Cathedral was, in fact, based on solutions derived from international experiments of the late 14th century. Priority was given to French and German models. In the panorama of late 14th century Italian architecture, Milan Cathedral features as an example of an instance where models were imported that had little to do with solutions that had been tried and tested in other Italian building yards. The sole traditional element utilised was the proportional ratio between the height of the nave and the aisles — but the opportunity to dispense with flying buttresses was not siezed, indeed, the preference was rather to multiply them by adopting a system of double flying and double vertical buttresses with turrets and pinnacles. Together with the external vertical buttresses, the huge windows and the profusion of sculptures and ornament, these are all elements that recall French Flamboyant architecture.

opposite page
External view of the choir of Milan Cathedral, begun 1387, Italy

The cathedral was completed during the 19th century with the plan layout of the façade and the spire. The cathedral preserves its original areas on the eastern end — the wide polygonal choir lit by historic stained glass windows.

CRACOW AND POLAND

Poland's connections with the German Empire during the 13th century were weak and with France weaker still. Even so, the number of Gothic buildings constructed seems quite significant, especially as for the most part, the cities, among them Krakow, were reformed in the 13th century according to German law and promoted buildings that recall Cistercian and Burgundian antecedents.

Indeed, art history stresses the role of Cistercian architecture in the shaping of Polish Gothic, starting with the stone and brick cathedral on the Wawel in Cracow. This cliff overhanging the River Vistula, is the political and religious centre of the city. The urban structure of Cracow was on a par with that of Prague. It, too, was the capital of a kingdom with a cathedral built over the tomb of the patron saint — St Stanislaus — positioned on the top of a hill within the walls of the Royal Palace together with an ancient and reputed university, founded by King Casimir the Great in 1364.

South elevation of Cracow Cathedral, c. 1333–1370, Poland

Cracow Cathedral — founded in the Romanesque period on the Wawel — was the inauguration and the final resting place of Polish kings. Between 1333 and 1370, it would undergo important restorations at the behest of King Casimir the Great. It is a brick structure with stone quoins and ornamental courses built round the tomb of St Stanislaus. The original architectural style of the cathedral is obscured on the exterior by successive reworking. This includes the Renaissance chapel of St Sigismund — with its two gilded cupolas — that is the burial place of kings and queens. The two towers of the façade date back to the 16th and 17th centuries.

opposite page
Courtyard of the Collegium Maius, 1492–1497, Cracow, Poland

The ancient Jagellonian University of Cracow possesses one of the few medieval university buildings still intact in continental Europe. Built by Master Johann, the courtyard has highly original architectural features. The buildings are arranged around a porticoed courtyard, one of the earliest north of the Alps, with a walkway and a deeply projecting roof. Some of the details, like the pillars carved with geometric motifs, can be compared with Late Gothic Austrian churches.

**Marienburg Castle (Malbork),
1270 –15th century, Poland**

Considered one of the greatest Gothic castles in Europe and built as the principal residence of the Teutonic Order — seat of Grand Master Siegfried von Feuchtwangen and administrative centre after the transfer from Venice — Marienburg Castle combined the functions of a monastery, a fortress and a palace. The fortress is built on the River Nogat and consists of two main sections in addition to the large defensive structure, the upper castle and the middle part linked to the castle via a bridge.

The upper castle is surrounded by deep ditches and various enclosing walls in order to guard the chapter room, the church of Our Lady and the chapel of St Anna, which acted as the sepulchre for the Grand Masters of the order. The middle castle housed visiting knights from Western Europe and included the great refectory and the infirmary. The palace of the Grand Master — on the left of the picture — is situated in the southwest corner rising above the walls.

ENGLISH PERPENDICULAR

From the reign of Edward III (begun 1430s), English architecture took a decisive step forward in the quest for new qualities of space. Clients preferred elegant forms and were unscrupulous in enhancing their elite status within a fairly dynamic social framework. The growing wealth of the great landowners and the higher ranks of the church and state hierarchies meant that opportunities for progress were created precisely within the ambit of initiatives that Church and monarchy promoted.

The term 'Perpendicular' or 'Rectilinear Style' refers to the structural arrangements used for the walls — based on the framework of an orthogonal grid — consisting of slender vertical and horizontal members. These are accompanied by other decorative elements that further enrich the rhythmic pattern: series of narrow columns, pointed arches, rose windows, racemes, quatrefoils, etc. The shape of the vaults and their related supports — as well as their interrelationships — was ground for experimentation and became the central focus of the new style. From this time on, local, independent solutions appeared in England that were truly eclectic and unorthodox in character, explicitly challenging practices of French provenance — for instance, the angles of glazed walls, flying buttresses and fan-vaulting. Although at this time new English architecture really only amounted to extensions and completions of existing buildings, this form of Gothic elaborated ever more original and fantastic shapes. Perpendicular Gothic corresponded as perfectly to the exigencies of religious architecture as to other areas of building, setting up an interesting and stimulating exchange of experimentation among various sectors of construction activity.

opposite page
Henry Yevele, cloister of Canterbury Cathedral, c. 1380, England

The cloister of Canterbury Cathedral features some of the most innovative forms in the Perpendicular Style. It is built as a close-knit series of funnel-shaped fan-vaulting, further enriched with subordinate ribs and abundant decorative reliefs that transfigure the ancient ogival vaults.

The fan-vaulting was a new structural system composed of ribs that generated a conical shape tangential to the cone, formed by the pillar opposite. This was a technical advance of some importance, as it placed the structural and those more specifically decorative elements conceptually on the same plane.

William Ramsey, choir of Gloucester Cathedral, c. 1337–1360, England

Gloucester Cathedral is the first clear example of the new architectural era, achieving effects of transparency, dematerialisation, a sense of unreality, imaginative tension and a striking treatment of the walls in the Perpendicular grid with which the architect, William Ramsey, enclosed the old choir. The vault is covered with a fine mesh of liernes, while three parallel ribs indicate the median axis.

THE MASTERPIECE
KING'S COLLEGE CHAPEL, CAMBRIDGE

During the 15th and 16th centuries, alongside the extraordinary developments of church architecture, secular architecture, too, experienced a glorious period no less spectacular. The interests of the English crown in the cities of Cambridge and Oxford, where the two most important universities were established, ensured that the building of the university infrastructure and the colleges received special attention. Technically challenging and grandiose, King's College Chapel — begun in 1446 by Reginald Ely and completed by John Wastell between 1508 and 1515 — may be considered to epitomise the Perpendicular Style. The structure of the cathedral is linked to similar technical and formal experiments already attempted in religious buildings. Extremely high walls were completely replaced by large window surfaces and the masonry of the lower part was transformed into a lofty covering of delicately latticed tracery. The extreme verticality of the interior is enhanced by slender shafts, which lead the gaze upwards to the heavenly vaults. Built in the early 16th century, King's College is a masterpiece of the art of vaulting in its consistent use of the quintessentially English interpretation of the fanvault. This type of vault, introduced as early in the late 14th century in the cloisters of Gloucester and Canterbury and, up until then, used only to cover small areas, was used extensively here achieving technical and formal brilliance, where the tracery of the windows is extended all the way up to the roof itself.

External view of King's College Chapel, begun 1466, Cambridge, England

The exterior of King's College Chapel shows a simple rectangular floor plan layout and clear volumetric masses — an elongated parallelepiped that employs a castellar structure which goes beyond the functional requirements of the building.
The corner turrets, similar to those of English castles, frame an impressive façade dominated, as per usual, by an enormous window. The side elevations are punctuated by a close sequence of buttresses, accommodating the large window openings.

opposite page
View of the vault of King's College Chapel, 1508–1515, Cambridge, England

This vault is a masterpiece, not only due to its exquisite formal qualities, but also due to its achievement from a technical point of view. The fanvaults in King's College Chapel are not built in a traditional way with separated ribs and sails, but are constructed from chiselled stone plates of considerable weight.

THE MASTERPIECE
WESTMINSTER ABBEY, HENRY VII'S CHAPEL

The last of the magnificent series of royal chapels, concluding medieval architecture in England arrived with the alteration of the former Lady Chapel of Westminster Abbey into a royal burial chapel by Henry VII, equalling in scale to a separate church in its dimensions. Built between 1503 and 1519, the surface of its walls, both inside and out, is completely covered with small panels. The crowning architectural glory of the chapel is the vault, which is modelled on that at King's College, Cambridge. Robert and William Vertue created a pendant fan-vault ceiling; its particular pattern of curve and counter-curve confers a decorative richness to the whole ensemble.

The overall impression is that individual elements of the vault have almost completely lost their structural function. The nave is marked by ornate transverse arches, which seem to vanish into the central part of the roof to be absorbed into the profile of the pendants arranged in three rows — the central arch follows the main thrust of the nave with two symmetrical arches at either side. Nonetheless, the abundant amount of light radiating from the great windows remodels the rich decorative intricacy and endows the whole with a unified architectural validity whose results are perfectly in keeping with the symbolic and exemplary requirements of court ceremony. With the construction of Henry VII Chapel, medieval English architecture reached its final chapter.

opposite page
Cross-section showing the elevation and design of the structural system of the vault of Henry VII's Chapel, 1503–1519, Westminster Abbey, London, England

The structural technique that makes this masterpiece at all feasible is not visible; the transverse supporting arches disappear after a short initial distance, distributing their weight on to the external buttresses.

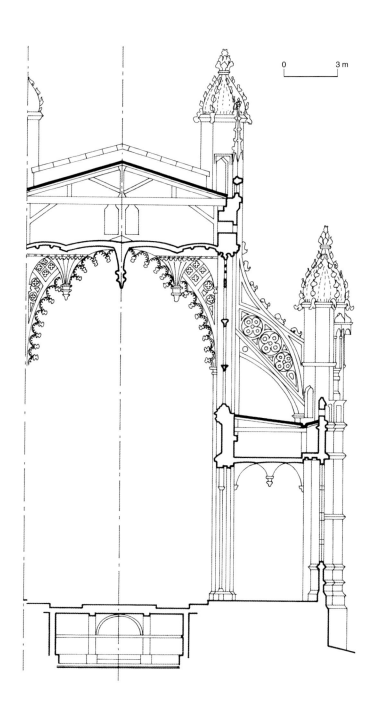

0   3 m

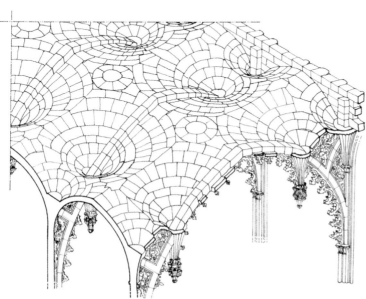

**Vault of Henry VII's Chapel,
1503–1519, Westminster Abbey,
London, England**

The main concept of English Late
Gothic was the systematic use of fan-
vaulting, a solution already previously
attempted. Late Gothic in England
found evermore refined development
in combination with components of
pendant vaults, creating spatial
effects evoking of a kind of forest of
branches or a cave of stalactites.

FLANDERS AND BRABANT

The accelerated development of international relations in Flanders and Brabant, not only in commerce, manufacturing (especially of textiles and wool)
and finance, but also in artistic and cultural matters, had already greatly stimulated civic life from the end of the 13th century, triggering a marked development in the sphere of public building works. The birth of an economic and
political oligarchy, keen to portray an impression of itself that would match
such wealth, caused the new urban middle classes to promote the construction of splendid buildings that, from the 14th century, would frequently be
distinguished by their rich architectural decoration and their use of fine freestone masonry.
The most demanding undertakings — in addition to the city walls — con-
cerned the *hallen* and the town halls. The former, hallen, were also used as
warehouses for merchandise and meeting places for the community. The latter, town halls, were already administrative centres in the modern sense of
the word. Political prestige, moreover, required a high urban profile, thus leading to an extraordinary proliferation of towers on the *hallen*, town halls and
churches, that all came to have similar uses. The towers increasingly resem-
bled each other in typology — rising from a square base to terminate in an octagon.
Initially church architecture was influenced by the great French cathedrals,
especially in the border areas; though in a simplified form. The church Gothic architecture of Brabant was in fact a variant of 14th and 15th century Euro-

bottom left
Begijnhof, c. 1240, Ghent, Belgium

Ghent is the capital of the old county
of East Flanders and was an important
centre of manufacturing, in continual
competition with Bruges. Ghent has
three béguinages sisterhoods: the old
and the new Béguinage of St Elizabeth
and that of Our Lady, Ter Hooyen.

bottom right
**Tower of St Martin's Cathedral,
1254–1517, Utrecht, Netherlands**

The churches in Flanders and Brabant
were also attributed municipal functions, which explains the gigantic 'sky-
scraper' form given to façade towers.
The towers were not only an emblem
of the city and its inhabitants, but also
served as watchtowers.
The tower in Utrecht became a prototype for many others around the country — a single tower 112m high does
not easily combine with the plan of a
cathedral, but must nevertheless have
greatly impressed contemporaries.

pean architecture deliberately combining French and English elements, whilst rejecting the complicated vaulting that was being widely built, as the sobre middle class oligarchy, who were among the builders of collegiate and parish churches, rejected it.

A special aspect of Flemish culture was the institution of the *begijnhof*- (Beguines), a lay sisterhood of pious single women and widows who took vows of poverty, chastity and obedience. Originating in the province of Liège at the end of the 13th century, the sisterhood spread into Flanders especially. It sprang up spontaneously at the time of the Crusades, when the men were setting off for the Holy Land with little likelihood of coming back. Noblewomen — disdaining marriage with men of lower rank — grouped together in small communities on the outskirts of the towns, with their own parish church, parish priest and cemetery. Surrounded by high walls, access to the béguinage was by a door that was bolted at night. Badly esteemed by the Church, beguines and begards (the masculine equivalent) were accused of interpreting sacred scripture too freely, of reading the Bible in their vernacular and of neglecting the sacraments to such an extent that they were soon persecuted by the Inquisition and condemned as heretics by the Council of Vienna in 1311. After this date, the béguinages slowly fell apart, until the institution finally dissolved completely.

View of the city of Ghent, Belgium

Ghent, Chief city of East Flanders, showed a consistent increase in its population due to its economic prosperity and its successful mercantile trade. The city had to raise the level of its embankments in order to adapt to the new demands of river traffic linking it with the port of the Zwin at Damme. The bridge spanning the river, alongside excellent Late Gothic palaces, is constructed in the prized blue stone of Tournai and led to the Church of St Nicholas that stands out among the houses because of the bulk of its great crossing tower. The large windows in the façade seem to echo English models.

BRUGES

The city of Bruges was governed by an economic oligarchy who controlled the production and export of woollen fabric to the whole of Europe. Through its splendid public buildings Bruges asserted its feeling of civic pride and independence from the great European powers on its borders — France and the Empire.

The old city, centred on two distinct focal points: the Market Square and the Burg Square — which was overlooked by the town hall and the church of the Holy Blood — still entirely surrounded by canals formerly used to transport merchandise, has managed to preserve its medieval appearance intact.

The 14th century town hall (Stadhuis) was the prototype for all the succeeding municipal buildings built between the 15th and 16th centuries in Ghent, Arras and Brussels.

Nearby was the massive quadrilateral of the *hallen*, which covered an entire block. In the centre of its façade stood an imposing tower (belfry) destroyed by fire in 1280 and completely rebuilt at the end of the 13th century. The belfry had a double function in the Flemish area. On one hand, it was a symbol *par excellence* of civic pride and of the city's power — built to the greatest height possible so as to be seen from afar in the surrounding flat countryside — while on the other hand it housed the charters recording the emancipation of the free Flemish cities.

Begijnhof, c. 1230, Bruges, Belgium

The béguinage sisterhood of Bruges is one of the most important examples still preserved to the present day. The buildings of the béguinage are excellent examples of residential architecture in Flanders at the time. Urban dwellings were built on long and narrow building sites, between two parallel walls. The frame structure of the dwellings is infilled with bricks; the roofs are double-pitched.

St Jan's Hospital, 1188, Bruges, Belgium

Alongside the more famous public buildings such as the town hall and *hallen*, hospitals and welfare foundations were built in the ancient cities of the Low Countries. The hospital of St Jan, whose rear overlooks the canal, has an important sculptured façade linked iconographically with the Marian cult of the nearby church of Notre-Dame.

Stadhuis (Town Hall), 1377–1387, Bruges, Belgium

The Stadhuis was one of the first buildings in the Flemish area built in the Flamboyant Gothic style. Particular attention was paid to the decorative elements and especially to the form and distribution of the tall lanceolate windows placed over the bottom row of cruciform windows. This emphasises the vertical nature of the façade. The masonry surfaces are amply decorated, from the mouldings around the doorways to the mock battlements of the roof, the corner bartisans with their slender spires to the rich sculptural ornamentation (a great amount of which has unfortunately been lost or destroyed).

FRANCE PRIVATE DWELLINGS (HÔTELS)

The most important buildings in French Late Gothic architectural culture were ecclesiastical. However, there was no lack of important, innovative examples of secular building, both private and public. In this context, the private *hôtel* spread through France. The *hôtel* was a building typology configured around a courtyard, protected in turn by a high wall with an imposing entrance. It was usually built on two levels, preferably in natural stone and always featured several components: imposing turrets projecting out from the roof, corner turrets, pitched roofs with a series of dormer windows and stair towers that also extended beyond the roofs, situated in the corner positions in the courtyard. In a clergyman's house there would also be a chapel.

Rarely was there any consistency of compositional alignment or balance of masses and floors. Asymmetrical façades were favoured, with openings that corresponded to the internal arrangements of the rooms and were adapted to the irregularities of the urban layout. The façades usually featured rich external decoration, with profiled cornices framing windows and doors and skylights with broken pediments. There are two wonderful examples of this once-widespread building typology that survive, both are residences of leaders of the clergy: Hôtel de Cluny and Hôtel de Sens.

opposite page
Courtyard, Hôtel de Cluny,
1485–1498, Paris, France

The Hôtel de Cluny, erected by Abbot Jacques d'Amboise, is the oldest example of a private urban *hôtel*-type residence with a courtyard and garden. The double-storey building, with slate roof and large dormers, consists of the main block with two wings enclosing the courtyard. In the boundary wall separating the building from the city, there is only a gate (the former carriage entry) and a pedestrian entrance. Inside, the original arrangement of the rooms has been maintained, at least as regards their dimension. The orientation of the entrance and chapel have also been maintained.

Hôtel de Cluny was both the residence of the abbots of Cluny as well as the Cluniac college in Paris, i.e. guest quarters and a reception building. It is notable for the strong emphasis on detail in the Flamboyant Style — cruciform windows, entrance doorways surmounted with architectural decoration, a rib-vaulted portico, slender corner columns and gargoyles decorated with fantastic zoomorphic and plant motifs. At each corner there are circular turrets reminiscent of contemporary forms of fortified architecture.

Fireplace, Hôtel de Jacques Cœur,
1443–1453, Bourges, France

The great reception hall on the ground floor shows all the attributes of medieval ceremonial rooms. The monumental fireplace was rebuilt after the war in accord with documentary sources and surviving fragments.

CATALONIA AND ARAGON

Towards the end of the 13th century in regions ruled by the crown of Aragon (including Catalonia and the Balearic Islands), Spanish Gothic entered its next phase. Parallel to similar experimental solutions in southern France, there was a tendency to structure the interior of buildings in order to make a wide unified space extending in every direction. The new buildings rejected the tight succession of spaces and clear separation of the bay as a generative module encountered in Castilian cathedrals, dissolving the material consistency of masonry surfaces and ignoring the load-bearing structure whether real or illusory.

The Pyrenean frontier area, thus continued to be one of the most proactive in devising innovative spatial experiments of high formal and constructional quality — which would open the way for the great Majorcan churches — via a conjunction of factors ranging from the persistence of local Romanesque traditions to the massive presence of the mendicant orders. In parallel, during the 13th and 14th centuries, cloisters would become an integral part of church buildings and, in the splendid tracery that decorated the colonnades, unbridled fantasy was given free rein, with overt echoes of motifs from Moorish tradition.

A flourishing maritime trade sustained this extraordinary artistic development in Catalonia and the Balearics. The entire economic prosperity of the kingdom depended on this trade, as did urban culture and the exchange of

opposite page
Berenguer de Montagut, Ramon Despuig, Guillem Metge, choir and axonometric of the church of St Maria del Mar, 1328–1383, Barcelona, Catalonia

St Maria del Mar is a parish church, commissioned by ship owners and merchants in order to rival the largest city churches. The church is built according to a square pattern (floor plan and elevation inscribed in a regular parallelepiped) and features an open, expansive interior — a typical hall church, i.e. nave and aisles of almost equal height and no transept, with slender octagonal pillars (1) which do not obscure the overall lines of sight, with a crossing vault (2). The architect adopted a geometric solution for the aisles with their chapels, which follow the line and enclose the choir (3). The remarkable verticality of this space is accentuated even more by the use of an exact system of mathematical proportions.

Guglielmo Sagrera, façade of La Llotja, 1426–1446, Palma di Majorca, Spain

La Llotja is characteristic of Catalan architecture — an assembly room for merchants, as well as a sort of stock exchange for maritime activities. The building in Palma is notable for the contrast between its simple external scale — a kind of massive block on a rectangular base with corner towers, built near the sea in perfect harmony with its surroundings — and the structure of the great internal hall, subdivided by two rows of twisted pillars which bear the weight of the vault.

people and ideas between Spain and Italy. The mercantile middle class played a primary role in patronage of the arts in Catalan cities.

Catalan-Aragonese culture, although apparently rooted in the European Gothic tradition, departed from it, giving rise to unexpected results, whether by adhering to motifs anchored in Romanesque practices or by the careful choice of contemporary Gothic elements imbued with local influences.

The great attention paid to civic and buildings for the intelligentsia in the 14th and 15th centuries was important. The development of parliament buildings and town halls can be related to the early expansion of civic institutions in the entire Catalan dominion — as well as commercial and military buildings. In these, the quest for new themes and spatial values were given ample opportunity to develop independently with original results.

This development distanced the dominion evermore clearly from other Iberian areas, as Catalan-Aragonese influence spread beyond the Peninsula, from the Balearic Islands to Sicily and from Sardinia to the State of Naples.

The prevailing objective of Catalan construction in its great halls was to evolve spaces, volumes and structural details inspired by a great clarity and conciseness, using a building system which covered great rooms with wooden ceilings supported by diaphragm arches. Structural solutions that avoided the use of flying buttresses were preferred. Together with a refined combination of rectilinear geometric grids and flowing lines, a general sobriety of aesthetic guided structural and expressive choices.

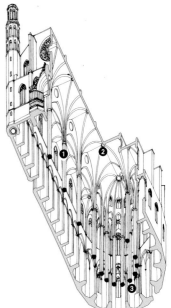

South side of the cathedral of Palma di Majorca, begun c. 1300, Spain

Begun around the year 1300 — with the east end completed in 1327 — the building of the cathedral was resumed about the middle of the century as a modified scheme aiming at gigantism. The structure of the southern section uses a system of buttresses and double flying arches, completed by masonry partitions placed orthogonally in the axis of the main corpus, their function being to lighten the wall masses and take the thrust of the vaults. At the level of the side chapels, there is a secondary, lesser order of elongated buttresses almost the height of reinforcing turrets. The thickening of the buttressing partitions in the lower order transforms it into a solid wall of fluted stone with strong lines of shade-producing chiaroscuro effects.

opposite page
La Llotja, interior, c. 1380–1392, Barcelona, Catalonia

The great hall has a rectangular layout, arranged on a system with large diaphragm arches supporting the roof. This building is considered one of the main examples of Catalan Gothic — both for its specific architectural value and also as it encompasses many of the morphological characteristics of secular Catalan-Aragonese buildings.

ISABELLINE GOTHIC IN SPAIN

Between the 15th and 16th centuries, architectural output in the Iberian peninsula was enormous and varied, reflecting a set of events that brought about profound changes throughout the Mediterranean basin — the union of the two kingdoms of Castile and Aragon and the consequent creation of a powerful politico-territorial entity. These changes included: the significant acceleration of the centuries-old process of the *Reconquista*; the election of Spanish Cardinal, Rodrigo Borgia, to the Papal throne; the political enlargement of trade routes and the geographic explorations that would bring about the discovery of America by Europeans in 1492.

In this climate, a process of intense architectural progress evolved, creating important works which revealed the presence of features recognisably drawn from local traditions. The numerous cathedrals built in Spanish cities throughout the 15th century and beyond, were an expression of this revival, constructed in response to politico-religious and territorial considerations.

At the close of the century, there was a further development — the formation of the Isabelline Style — considered an extreme variant of the Late Gothic idiom. This style embraced aspects of Flamboyant Gothic, imparted with Mudejar elements and even featuring Renaissance traits. Created for the court, Isabelline Style took the form of a rich and splendid aesthetic laden with decorative features, clearly illustrating the politico-religious character of the cultural and architectural choices of Isabel and Ferdinand.

opposite page
Juan Guas, cloister of San Juan de los Reyes, c. 1479–1480, Toledo, Spain

An important work built in an Isabelline Style, San Juan de los Reyes commemorates the victory of the Reyes Católicos in 1476 and accommodates a royal mausoleum. The great cloister is distinguished by the rich decoration of pillars and buttresses alongside the filigree openwork and the broken curves of the arches of the upper gallery.

Vault of the Vélez Chapel, 1490–1507, Murcia Cathedral, Spain

The quest for monumentality in Spanish architecture of the 15th–16th centuries is apparent in the great funerary and votive chapels, generally built on a central plan close to great cathedrals. The Vélez family chapel has an irregular octagonal plan with a star vault.

Portal of the University, c. 1525, Salamanca, Spain

Ecclesiastical colleges or universities were built between the 15th and 16th centuries at Valladolid and Salamanca in western Spain. In the lavish ornamentation of the portal at Salamanca, an early stronghold of Renaissance humanism, Gothic forms mingle with Italianate elements in a Plateresque Style whose decorative genre is comparable, both in structure and contents, with monumental Spanish retables. Typical of these elements is the union of walls and framed surfaces, rather like an oversized exhibit. The architecture becomes secondary: the wall is decorated with an overt allegorical programme promoting the role of the Spanish monarchy, which presented itself as a bulwark of the faith, promoter of sciences and conqueror of vice.

Casa de las Conchas (House of the Shells), 1512, Salamanca, Spain

In the 15th and 16th centuries, secular architecture in Spain was especially rich in ostentatious urban aristocratic townhouses. The lavish external decoration of the Casa de las Conchas unites several traditional Spanish-Moorish elements with naturalism typical of the Late Gothic period. In 15th century Salamanca a taste for the style called Plateresque, which combined Late Gothic themes with other classical motifs as well as those drawn from nature, became widespread. This trend in Spanish decorative taste is perhaps akin to the fashion in Italy at that time for naturalistic decoration, such as artificial rocks and grottoes, ornamental incrustation with real shells, gravel and pebbles.

Juan and Rodrigo Gil de Hontañón, exterior (top) and view of the vaults of the presbytery (left) of the new Cathedral of Salamanca, begun 1513, Spain

According to modern criteria already used (for example in Milan), the trend was to summon the most well-renowned architects of the period when it involved a prestigious building, such as was the case in the new cathedral of Salamanca. At that time the city had reached the peak of its glory and its demographic development, with its university among the foremost in Europe. Among the commissioned architects was Juan de Hontañón, who was succeeded after his death by his son, Rodrigo in 1538. In 1513 the architect commenced work on the structure of the old cathedral, which was no longer adequate for the city's needs. He started with the façade, reducing the length of the north aisle and adding a row of side chapels to each aisle. The side chapels were situated between buttresses, which gave the impression of a church with double aisles of gradually reducing height.

Rodrigo finished the star vaults and the crowning glory of the façade, making a decisive turn towards a Hispano-Flamenca version of Late Gothic that tended to emphasise the calligraphic or linear components, conferring monumentality on the exterior and creating light, pleasant, grandiose interiors. He introduced a style of balustrades, rectangular and circular windows (oculi) as well as Plateresque ornamentation. The persistence of 'antique' forms is illustrated by the fact that once work had been suspended for financial reasons, controversy was still raging as to how the transept and the apsidal area should be completed. In the event, Gothic would prevail over the Renaissance.

Inside, the great height of the building, with its wide aisles, gives an impression of grandeur, harmony and richness of decoration. The shafts of the clustered piers soar almost uninterruptedly to richly moulded star vaults. The piers represent the unique, but refined, ornament of an overtly aesthetic style.

MANUELINE ARCHITECTURE IN PORTUGAL

The transition from Romanesque to authentic Gothic features occurred quite late in Portugal. Throughout the 14th century, building activity followed at a slow pace, its first boost provided by John I's ascent to the throne in 1385, which gave rise the artistic period known to history as the Johannine Style. From the mid-14th century, Portuguese building tradition continued to follow techniques and lexical features based on pointed arches and ogival crossing vaults in accordance with European Late Gothic. At the close of the 15th century, with the ascent of Manuel I the Fortunate (1495–1521) to the Portuguese throne, a remarkable period of expansion and splendour began, boosted by the impressive series of new settlements in the Far East and on the American continent. At this time, the characteristics of a new architectural phase developed in Portugal known as the Manueline Style. Between the 15th and 16th centuries, completely new codes and idioms were evolved. These codes were increasingly influenced by naturalistic or maritime imagery (anchors, scallops, ropes, sextants, armillary spheres etc.) — elements emblematic of the Portuguese Empire, since they referred to the development of navigation, geographic discoveries and economic expansion. The Manueline Style was typified by its eclecticism and has been interpreted as a phase of transition to the new Renaissance culture which spread widely into Portugal. This development occurred thanks to a process of infiltration of, and combination with, innovative Renaissance traits, marked by a light-hearted setting, freed from the pressure of creating new themes and stylistic symbols.

opposite page
Francisco de Arruda, Belém Harbour Tower, 1510–1520, Lisbon, Portugal

The tower — built of entirely of freestone — stands directly on the coast at the mouth of the Tagus River and is an icon of Manueline Late Gothic. It consists of two sections: a low covered base with a terrace and the tower proper, which combines elements of several morphological origins. The tower has arrangements typical of military architecture such as projecting bartisans, gun ports and crenelated battlements with merlons and walkways. It is also notable for its decorative motifs, which incorporate new formal European developments typical of the 16th century: small cupolas, the use of coats of arms and nautical forms deriving from sea-faring activities typical of Portugal. Functionally, the building had more of a prestigious than strategic function.

Diego Boytac, João Castilho, Diego de Torralba Monastery of the Hieronymites of Belém, begun 1502, Lisbon, Portugal

The creation of the magnificent complex at the gates of Lisbon — in a significant location from where naval expeditions would set out — was promoted by King Manuel and entrusted to the architect, Boytac. The building works were taken over by João Castilho in 1517 and subsequently by Diego de Torralba, who completed it around 1572. The final two architects who worked on the monastery decisively modified the Portuguese Style of the 16th century by introducing several Renaissance elements, which gave the signal for a change towards the classical culture, by that time widespread throughout Europe.
If the establishment was already unusual, even more noteworthy was the formal classification of various architectural elements reminiscent of motifs drawn from the vegetable and animal worlds (leaves, shells, ropes) in a persistent search for naturalistic and nautical motifs.

THE MASTERPIECE
THE CONVENT OF SANTA MARIA DA VITORIA, BATALHA

The Dominican convent of Santa Maria da Vitoria, was commissioned by John I to commemorate the 1385 Battle of Aljubarrota and Portugal's consequent independence and was built by the architects, Alfonso Domingues and Huguet. The convent consists of the church and three magnificent cloisters, which accommodate stylistic components of diverse provenance. French elements appear in the high longitudinal corpus and in the external decorative details typical of Flamboyant Gothic. The layout of the vaults, with their extra linear ribs (liernes) and the horizontal arrangement of the façade, echo features of English Gothic origin, both Curvilinear Decorated and Perpendicular. Santa Maria da Vitoria might not be the most significant work of Portuguese architecture, but is perhaps the monument that best embodies the demand in the zeitgeist of the time for a progression toward Gothic architecture. It should also be remembered that the convent was founded on unusual premises, as it as a product of a royal initiative, which, through architecture, affirmed a principle of political legitimisation in a message mainly addressed to the populace. Furthermore, Santa Maria da Vitoria is a work which — with its expression of international components — expresses and symbolises the idea and political programme of the king and his relationship with an older tradition of monarchies.

opposite page
Alfonso Domingues, royal cloister of the monastery of Santa Maria da Vitoria, late 14th century, tracery by Diego Boytac, c. 1500, Batalha, Portugal

The cloister is distinguished by pointed arches with white marble infill in the Manueline Style to create *celosias* (pierced stone lattice-work decorations). The style of the cloister is based on Manueline architecture and 'oceanic Gothic', which flourished in Portugal in the 15th–16th centuries.

Huguet, western façade of the monastery of Santa Maria da Vitoria, 15th century, Batalha, Portugal

Huguet, a master builder — possibly of English origins — created the west façade of the monastery, where the magnificent doorway and the Flamboyant window above it are framed by the linear decoration of the central section. At the sides, a complex arrangement of flying buttresses absorbs the thrust of the vaulting.

INDEX OF PLACES

Aachen (Germany), 9, 97
Aigues-Mortes (France), 46, 69
Albi (France), 69, 71, 72, 100
Amiens (France), 7, 13, 29, 44, 49, 50, 62, 63
Annaberg (Germany), 110
Assisi (Italy), 35, 86
Auxerre (France), 49
Avignon (France), 68, 70, 84
Barcelona (Spain), 130, 132
Batalha (Portugal), 10, 140
Beaune (France), 16
Beauvais (France), 13, 25
Bologna (Italy), 19, 84, 90
Bourges (France), 24, 35, 40, 44, 46, 49, 128
Bruges (Belgium), 14, 124, 126, 127
Burgos (Spain), 9, 74, 75
Caernarvon (Wales), 46
Cambridge (England), 120, 122
Canterbury (England), 22, 24, 42, 78, 118, 120
Carcassonne (France), 72, 73
Castel del Monte (Italy), 97
Chartres (France), 7, 26, 31, 36, 44, 49, 56, 60
Chorin (Germany), 64
Colmar (France), 18
Cologne (Germany), 9, 10, 58, 60, 62, 63, 81, 108
Conques (France), 24
Cracow (Poland), 114
Ely (England), 76, 120
Ferrara (Italy), 82, 83
Florence (Italy), 11, 14, 17, 50, 84, 89, 90, 93
Ghent (Belgium), 124, 125, 126
Gloucester (England), 101, 118, 120
Kutná Hora (Czech Republic), 108, 109
Laon (France), 7, 13, 20, 36
León (Spain), 9, 53, 74
Limburg an der Lahn (Germany), 58
Lincoln (England), 40, 78
Lisbon (Portugal), 138
London (England), 7, 76, 122, 123
Lübeck (Germany), 17, 64, 66
Marienburg/Malbork (Poland), 116
Meissen (Germany), 100
Milan (Italy), 10, 84, 109, 112, 137
Murcia (Spain), 134
Naumburg (Germany), 30, 31
Noyon (France), 7, 9, 24, 36
Orvieto (Italy), 83, 95
Padua (Italy), 89
Palma, Majorca (Spain), 16, 130, 132
Paris (France), 5, 7, 9, 13, 20, 24, 30, 35, 36, 53, 80, 98, 128
Perugia (Italy), 35, 86, 91
Piacenza (Italy), 88
Pisa (Italy), 84

Poblet (Catalonia), 39
Poitiers (France), 17
Pontigny (France), 38
Prague, (Czech Republic), 101, 104, 105, 106, 108, 114
Prenzlau (Germany), 64
Rheims (France), 7, 44, 50, 53, 58
Rievaulx (England), 39
Rodez (France), 68
Saint-Denis (France), 5, 26, 31, 36, 38, 42, 50, 53, 63
Saint-Germain-en-Laye (France), 53
Saint-Malo (France), 46
Salamanca (Spain), 136, 137
Salisbury (England), 24, 29, 31, 78
Schwäbisch Gmünd (Germany), 108
Seville (Spain), 10
Siena (Italy), 89, 94, 95
Soissons (France), 7, 24, 27, 53
Strasbourg (France), 10, 58, 60, 62, 108
Stralsund (Germany), 64
Syracuse (Italy), 96
Toledo (Spain), 9, 74, 134
Toulouse (France), 44, 49, 50, 68, 72, 74
Trier (Germany), 58
Utrecht (Holland), 124
Venice (Italy), 92, 93, 116
Vézelay (France), 7
Vienna (Austria), 21, 108
York (England), 78, 79, 80, 81
Wells (England), 28, 29, 76, 78, 81

PHOTOGRAPHIC CREDITS

Akg-images, Berlin: pp. 28, 32–33, 63
(above), 76, 99, 101 (left), 109 (right);
23, 81 (A.F. Kersting); 6, 8, 9, 10, 12–13,
14 (right), 24, 27, 29, 31, 34, 36 (left), 37,
38, 40, 43, 45, 47, 48, 51, 52, 61, 62, 64,
65, 67, 68, 77, 78, 79, 80, 100, 104, 105,
108, 109 (left), 111, 118, 119, 120, 121,
123 (above), 124 (left), 126, 127, 128, 131
(above), 132, 134, 136, 137 (above)
(Bilarchiv Monheim); 39 (left), 116–117
(Bildarchiv Steffens); 114 (David
Borland); 20 (Gilles Mermet); 60 (left)
(Hedda Eld); 15, 49, 57, 106, 129, 138,
139, 140, 141 (Hervé Champollion); 66,
107 (Hilbich); 30 (left) (Jean-Paul
Dumontier); 59 (Jost Schilgen); 74, 137
(below) (Paul M.R. Maeyaert); 39 (right)
(Richard Boot); 7 (Roman von Götz);
54–55, 70, 75, 82, 97, 124 (right), 125
(Schutze/Rodermann); 16, 58 (left)
(Stefan Drechsel); 110 (above)
(Werner Unfug)

Archives, Mondadori Electa, Milan: pp. 11,
14 (left), 17, 25 (below), 26, 36 (right),
41, 42, 53, 56 (left), 58 (right), 63
(below), 71 (right), 86, 87, 90 (above),
90 (below right), 92 (left), 110 (below),
112, 122, 123 (below), 131 (below); 84,
91, 94, 95 (Arnaldo Vescovo); 19, 96
(Marco Ravenna)

BAMSphoto di Basilio Rodella,
Montichiari (BS): p. 56 (right)

Bridgeman Art Library, London:
p. 25 (above)

Cameraphoto Arte, Venice: p. 92 (right)

© Corbis: pp. 130 (Andrea Jemolo);
93 (Angelo Hornak); 69 (Bertrand
Rieger); 46 (Christophe Boisvieux);
135 (Juan Gras); 88 (Massimo
Borchi); 72 (Patrick Ward); 133
(Peter Aprahamian); 71 (left)
(Will Pryce/Thames & Hudson/Arcaid)

Giorgio Deganello, Padua: p. 89

© Granataimages/Alamy: pp. 102–103

© Lessing/Contrasto: pp. 4, 30 (right),
101 (right), 109 (right), 115

Rabatti & Domingie, Florence: p. 50

Scala Group, Florence: pp. 90 (below)
(left), 113 (2006)

Front cover: The Chapter House vault, York Minster, c. 1290, see p. 79 (© akg, Berlin)
Back cover: The external façade of the Doge's Palace, Venice, Italy, 1422–1424, see p. 93
(© Angelo Hornak / CORBIS)

© 2011, Prestel Verlag, Munich, London, New York, for the English edition
© 2011 by Mondadori Electa SpA, Milan, for the original edition, all rights reserved

Prestel Verlag, Munich
A member of Verlagsgruppe Random House GmbH

Prestel Verlag
Neumarkter Strasse 28
81673 Munich
Tel. +49 (0)89 4136-0
Fax +49 (0)89 4136-2335

Prestel Publishing Ltd.
4 Bloomsbury Place
London WC1A 2QA
Tel. +44 (0)20 7323-5004
Fax +44 (0)20 7636-8004

Prestel Publishing
900 Broadway, Suite 603
New York, NY 10003
Tel. +1 (212) 995-2720
Fax +1 (212) 995-2733

www.prestel.com

Library of Congress Control Number is available;
British Library Cataloguing-in-Publication Data:
a catalogue record for this book is available from the
British Library; Deutsche Nationalbibliothek holds
a record of this publication in the Deutsche National-
bibliografie; detailed bibliographical data can be
found under: http://dnb.d-nb.de

Prestel books are available worldwide. Please
contact your nearest bookseller or one of the
above addresses for information concerning
your local distributor.

Editorial direction: Curt Holtz
Translation: Bridget Mason, Perth, Scotland
Copyediting: Anna Roos, Bern
Typesetting: Vornehm GmbH, Munich
Cover: Sofarobotnik, Augsburg & Munich
Production: Astrid Wedemeyer
Art direction: Cilly Klotz
Printing and binding: Mondadori Printing, Verona

Printed in Italy

ISBN 978-3-7913-4596-3

FSC
www.fsc.org
MIX
Paper from
responsible sources
FSC® C018290

Verlagsgruppe Random House FSC-DEU-0100
The FSC-certified paper Respecta Satin has
been supplied by Burgo cartiere (Italy).

723.5 P954   HBRAW
Prina, Francesca.
The story of Gothic architecture /

 BRACEWELL
 08/12